'Rich mix'

Inclusive strategies for urban regeneration

Sue Brownill and Jane Darke

The POLICY PRESS

First published in Great Britain in 1998 by

The Policy Press
University of Bristol
Rodney Lodge
Grange Road
Bristol BS8 4EA
UK

Tel no +44 (0)117 973 8797
Fax no +44 (0)117 973 7308
E-mail tpp@bristol.ac.uk
www.policypress.org.uk

© The Policy Press and the Joseph Rowntree Foundation, 1998

Reprinted October 2000

In association with the Joseph Rowntree Foundation

ISBN 1 86134 106 7

Photographs used on the front cover were supplied by Mo Wilson, Format Photographers, London and John Birdsall Photography, Nottingham.

Sue Brownill and **Jane Darke** both lecture at the School of Planning, Oxford Brookes University.

The title 'Rich mix' has been borrowed from a regeneration project of the same name in Tower Hamlets, East London. The Rich Mix Centre will be a national centre to celebrate London's cosmopolitan richness and show the contribution that migrant communities have made to developing and sustaining London's role as a world city. It will stimulate, foster and support intercultural understanding as well as providing a focus for community pride and identity; thereby contributing to breaking down barriers between communities, races, religions and geographical areas. For more information, please contact Nisar Ahmed on 020 7364 4075 or Andrew Bramidge 020 7377 5277.

The **Joseph Rowntree Foundation** has supported this project as part of its programme of research and innovative development projects, which it hopes will be of value to policy makers and practitioners. The facts presented and the views expressed in this report, however, are those of the authors and not necessarily those of the Foundation.

Cover design by Qube Design Associates, Bristol.
Printed in Great Britain by Hobbs the Printers Ltd, Southampton.

Contents

Acknowledgements

We would like to thank individuals from the following organisations who were interviewed for this report:

BTEG (Black Training and Enterprise Group)
Cityside SRB, Tower Hamlets
Commission for Racial Equality
Community Development Foundation
Ealing Family Housing Association
Government Office for the West Midlands
Green Street SRB, Newham
Heart of England TEC
Oxfam
Oxford City Council
Oxfordshire Ethnic Minority Business Service
West Midland Regional Development Network
Women's Design Service

We would also like to thank Konnie Razzaque for carrying out some of the interviews. We are grateful to the following for agreeing to be interviewed, providing considerable relevant material, or acting as critical readers of earlier drafts:

Audrey Bronstein, Roy Darke, John Low, Ines Smyth, Wendy Spray, Huw Thomas

In addition, we would like to acknowledge that we have used some material from shorter discussions with seminar participants, not named separately, and to thank those who attended.

The authors gratefully acknowledge financial support from the Joseph Rowntree Foundation.

Introduction

This report argues that genuine sustainable regeneration is impossible without an understanding of gender and of ethnic diversity, and that this aspect of regeneration should be brought from the margins to the mainstream. Policy and practice should be informed by a better operational understanding of how and why gender and race are relevant to the regeneration agenda and the benefits that flow from this.

Such an understanding starts from a recognition that areas undergoing regeneration are likely to show more diversity than most locations with respect to ethnic mix and family type, as households subject to discrimination and disadvantage are forced into areas with problems which are avoided by those who can choose. Just as the experience of social economic and political exclusion is likely to be different for men and women and for different minority groups, so routes to inclusion and regeneration will differ. That this is a *strategic* issue, raising questions about the direction and content of regeneration policies and their success in implementing their aims, is one of the major conclusions of this research.

This recognition of different routes to regeneration raises questions not only at the level of strategy but for the governance and implementation of urban policy. Practices at the interface between neighbourhoods and policy, such as consultation, delivery mechanisms and the drawing up of baseline data on regeneration areas, should all take account of diversity. At the strategic level the structure, membership and operation of partnerships and other regeneration agencies also carry implications for inclusion and exclusion.

This report argues that gender and ethnic diversity should not be seen as a *problem* for regeneration policies, agencies or professionals but as an *opportunity*. The 'rich mix' that results from such a perspective can release untapped resources and potential and assist in the process of sustainable regeneration. But we are not implying that this is without difficulties and conflicts as will be shown in later chapters.

The aims of the research

The aims of our research, which forms part of the Joseph Rowntree Area Regeneration Programme, were to:

- undertake a scene-setting review of existing policy and practice with respect to race and gender, based on a review of published work and secondary sources;

- identify strategic approaches which can best meet the aim of promoting wider equality of opportunity;

- identify best practice;

- consider future research and policy directions.

Gender and ethnicity: some issues

When this report uses the term 'minority ethnic groups', it must be understood that this refers to a range of groups of strongly contrasting economic situations and cultural norms. Some minorities are achieving economic success at the same or greater rate than the white majority. In all groups women face discrimination but the rules of behaviour for women and men that constitute 'gender' vary for the different ethnic groups. The social significance of being a man or a woman, and of membership of a particular ethnic group, is socially produced, contested and changing. Despite the existence of statistical patterns in the behaviour of different groups which may become the raw material for stereotyping, individuals from any background make choices about how to interpret and act on the 'rules' they learn from society.

This report often uses the term 'diversity' as shorthand to describe the mix of people in regeneration areas: of genders, ethnic groups, ages, skills, physical capacities and so on. Other terms such as social exclusion, inclusive regeneration and empowerment are also frequently used. The authors are conscious that these can come to be used as buzz words, in a way that forgets the complex realities they refer to rather than as summaries of this complexity. Readers are referred to the Glossary at the end of the report for a fuller discussion of these issues.

Urban policy

Issues of race, gender and other aspects of disadvantage have never been centre stage in urban policy. While race has often been on the policy agenda this has usually been implicit rather than explicit, and there has been little real analysis of how to address the issue. Urban policy has always lacked a specific analysis of gender, although recently there has been concern about the behaviour of young men, seen as prone to educational underachievement and crime in an economy that has no need for them. Yet policy and the ideology surrounding it has not been afraid to label minority ethnic populations or single parents as 'problems'. This stereotyped view limits the ability of regeneration policies to break down exclusion and may reinforce patterns of disadvantage.

There has been a tendency to see the communities on the receiving end of policies as *undifferentiated*, a tendency reflected in the lack of systematic research into the racial and gender dimensions of area regeneration. This latter aspect affected the aims of our research as we found that often we were in the position of reviewing a silence.

Urban policy has taken on many guises in the past 30 years and it is at present undergoing another of its regular metamorphoses. After almost two decades of belief in competition and trickle-down, issues of need and exclusion are once more on the agenda. There are therefore great opportunities for placing diversity at the core of regeneration policy. This optimism is reinforced by evidence of a new awareness of diversity in local initiatives, research and good practice which this and other research is beginning to reveal. Hopefully this momentum will continue so that people-led regeneration that is race- and gender-aware becomes a reality.

> Becoming people-led means, firstly, developing a thorough appreciation of the community's needs and aspirations and developing plans and programmes to match. This will mean recognising, and embracing, the diversity of needs within each community and being prepared to identify and work with all interests. (DoE, 1994)

The solutions to the problems such areas face cannot be found solely in policies aimed at those living in them. Wider issues about global and national economic processes, and national and local government policy in relation to issues such as education, health and housing all have their impact. Nevertheless the goal of sustainable regeneration cannot be met without a reorientation of policy, placing the issues of race and gender in the mainstream of area regeneration.

Methods

In carrying out this research we have concentrated on selectively reviewing existing work. This work has encompassed studies carried out under the Area Regeneration Programme and previous programmes of the Joseph Rowntree Foundation, and other publications both academic and from local government and the voluntary sector. It has been noticeable that over the short lifetime of the research project there has been a great increase in publications on these issues – which is encouraging but made our task harder. In addition we carried out a limited number of interviews with representatives from key organisations, including voluntary groups, government offices and researchers, listed in the Acknowledgements. We also held a seminar for research teams in the JRF Area Regeneration Programme and other researchers and practitioners which provided useful ideas and feedback. We would like to thank all those who contributed to the research while making the usual disclaimers about the views expressed being ours alone.

Structure of the report

Chapter 1 explains in greater detail why race and gender are issues in regeneration, discussing how poverty gives rise to economic, political and social exclusion. This chapter contains tables which present statistical evidence on the disadvantage experienced by most minority ethnic groups, and women, and shows some of the differences *between* the various ethnic groups (including whites). The diversity in economic positions, gender roles, family structures, and attitudes to other groups must be understood if the objectives of regeneration are to be achieved. Exclusion and poverty affect sections of society differently, so routes back into the mainstream of society must address the specific forms that exclusion may take.

Chapter 2 describes recent trends in urban policy including the rise of partnerships, and discusses how such structures may exclude. **Chapter 3** gives examples of projects which have had the vision to treat diversity as a strength. **Chapter 4** discusses several issues in the implementation of inclusive regeneration as well as the role of research. Finally, there is a summary, recommendations and conclusions.

The References and further reading lists the written sources used, highlighting the few that have any explicit engagement with the diverse nature of the communities in regeneration areas. A Glossary then discusses some of the words and phrases used in the report: many are shorthand terms for complex concepts. In the following Appendices we present various checklists from other reports that could be useful in race- and gender-aware regeneration policy and practice.

Postscript

Since this report was first printed in 1998 urban policy has inevitably moved on – particularly in the shape of new initiatives such as the New Deal for Communities and the National Strategy for Neighbourhood Renewal (SEU, 1998). These developments confirm the themes of exclusion, partnership and competitive bidding covered in the following pages. Many of the points made in this report are, therefore, still relevant when translated to the new policy context. Welcome new publications include the *New Deal for Communities: Race equality guidance* published by the DETR (2000) which responds to one original recommendation from this research for central government to take a lead in promoting equality.

Unfortunately we are unable to report similar initiatives in respect of gender, although exciting initiatives such as the West Midlands Women's Regeneration Network and the lottery-funded research by the Women's Design Service are happening at a local and regional level. We argue that all these developments point even more strongly to the need for adequate gender and race monitoring and auditing of urban policy. Our main argument – that diversity should be recognised as a strategic regeneration issue – remains constant despite this changing policy environment.

DETR (2000) *New Deal for Communities: Race equality guidance*, London: DETR, available at www.regeneration.detr.gov.uk/newdeal/race/guidance/index.htm

SEU (1998) *Bringing Britain together: A national strategy for neighbourhood renewal*, London: Cabinet Office, available at www.cabinet-office.gov.uk/seu/1998/bbt/nrhome.htm

Understanding race, gender and regeneration

This report argues that the diversity of experience among the population in areas on the receiving end of policy must lead to diverse routes to regeneration. Reviewing the regeneration literature leads to the inevitable conclusion that a monolithic view of regeneration is untenable. While there has been discussion on whether regeneration should be physical, social, holistic or sustainable, there has been inadequate attention to making it *inclusive*.

Accepting this conclusion brings with it major implications for policy and practice. But for those who are alarmed at the imagined complexity, conflict and time associated with this the answer is clear. Provided the structures are there, such as strategic policy aims, involvement in decision making and practices such as area profiling, participatory rapid appraisal, setting targets and monitoring, it *is* possible to achieve more inclusive regeneration. This report includes examples of what some initiatives are achieving. Rich mix refers, therefore, not only to the potential that can be released by accepting diversity as central to regeneration, but to the mix of tools and strategies available to policy and practice to meet this objective.

This chapter seeks to establish just why and how race and gender are central to regeneration. We examine some of the aspects of inclusive regeneration. The chapter goes on to discuss a major policy debate in inclusive regeneration: whether the targets set should be universal or specific to groups defined by gender and/or ethnicity.

Race, gender and the experience of regeneration

While recognising that race and gender are important concepts it is their expression in the everyday realities of living in regeneration areas and the making and implementing of policy that is of greater significance in understanding how and why they are vital to regeneration. Several studies show that not only are the problems regeneration policy seeks to address mediated by race and gender, they can also be the direct result of the operation of relations of gender and race and racism and sexism (May, 1997; Zahno, 1997). Policies, practices and systems of governance can be aware of this or by ignoring it they can deepen the inequalities that already exist (Loftman and Beazley, 1998).

Skelcher et al (1996, p 5) note four main themes in urban regeneration policy:

* enhancing the physical condition of localities;

* stimulating the local economy;

* tackling social and community issues;

* developing the longer-term future of the locality by strengthening the community's potential for self-government and by sustainable regeneration.

May (1997) and recent moves in government policy (DETR, 1997d) have placed combating poverty and social exclusion alongside these as a major objective for regeneration policy. Underlying all of them are issues of involvement, power and influence which are associated with the governance of regeneration policy. None of these can be fully understood without consideration of diversity, race and gender.

Poverty and social exclusion

Social exclusion is gaining widespread use as a term which recognises the broader impacts of material deprivation. Low income is bad enough in itself but it can bring with it exclusion from social, political, cultural and educational life. Geddes (1997) points out that social exclusion is a contested concept. Many are critical of its use as an evasive synonym for poverty. It may also collapse the diversity among those whose exclusion springs from different conditions: lone parents, unemployed people, minority ethnic groups, disabled people, those requiring care in the community. Its use can therefore mask the operation of racism and sexism.

Others see it as a way forward to place issues of race and gender at the mainstream of the regeneration agenda and to build bridges between areas often treated separately. Many feel the emphasis should be on *in*clusion as opposed to *ex*clusion as this locates the problem at its source, the factors of mainstream society that place some people and areas on the margins.

Whatever the discussions over the term, the evidence for recognising race and gender as major factors in poverty and exclusion is compelling. Women and ethnic minorities are more likely than average to be living in poverty and in areas targeted for regeneration projects. Further, men and women and people from different minority ethnic groups experience poverty and exclusion differently. If regeneration policy is to make "priorities associated with poverty and deprivation" central

(DETR, 1997a) these need to be taken into account.

Some basic facts stand out. May (1997) notes that 56% of adults on or below the income support level are women. Several studies show that statistics relating to poverty often stop at the front door and ignore the distribution of income within the family. Gender dynamics within the household often mean an unequal distribution of income within a household because of the assumptions that a male breadwinner has greater 'rights' to spend money. These assumptions persist even when the man is no longer the main breadwinner. Women often put the needs of their children in front of their own when it comes to spending money (Goode et al, 1998). Therefore anti-poverty strategies need to be aware that raising household income may not automatically increase the income of all household members.

Household structure also affects poverty for lone parents, the majority of which are women (see Table 1). While 63% of lone mothers have a gross weekly income of under £150 per week the figure for lone fathers is 34% and for other families 10% (ONS, 1997).

Poverty is also mediated by race and ethnicity. There is considerable diversity in unemployment rates between different ethnic groups: see Tables 2 and 3. These differences cannot be attributed to difference in educational qualifications.

A recent survey (Table 4; Modood, 1997) showed that while 28% of households who classified themselves as white had incomes less than half the national average the figures for Bangladeshi, Pakistani and Caribbean households were 84%, 82% and 41% respectively. This reflects a common pattern

Table 1: Income of lone parents and other families (%)

Gross weekly income	Lone mothers	Lone fathers	Other families
Up to £150	63	(34)	10
£150–£350	27	(35)	24
Over £350	10	(32)	65

Source: ONS (1997, Table 2.10) (Brackets in table signify small number of cases)

across a range of indicators that those who classify themselves as Indian, African Asian or Chinese are much closer to the economic position of white people than those of Caribbean, Pakistani or Bangladeshi descent. The growing number of refugees is adding to these dynamics.

Poverty is also a reflection of the operation of relations of race and gender (including discrimination) within the labour market (see Table 5). Women's weekly earnings are still only 73% of men's despite 20 years of equal opportunities legislation. Many studies have shown how women's responsibilities for childcare have led them to take career breaks, to take low paid part-time work or to not be able to work at all.

Women's participation in the labour force is also affected by ethnicity, with Caribbean women having levels of participation and average

weekly incomes above those for white women, while Pakistani and Bangladeshi women are generally working within the home. For men average levels of income for white, African Asian and Chinese are almost identical (£336 per week) while for Caribbean, Pakistani and Bangladeshi these are much lower (£306, £227 and £191 respectively) (Table 4).

Other issues are the greater likelihood of women and minority ethnic groups to be living in areas and tenures considered excluded (see Table 6). A total of 41% of Caribbean people and 28% of Pakistanis and Bangladeshis live in inner metropolitan areas compared to only 11% of the white population (Modood et al, 1997). These two ethnic groups also have higher than average numbers of people in social housing (Table 7). Lone parents, single women and divorced or separated women are also more likely to be living in social housing than men in the same category.

Table 2: ILO unemployment rates by ethnicity and gender

	Men	Women
White	8.9	6.0
Black Carribean	22.9	15.1
Black African	27.9	14.1
Indian	13.9	11.7
Pakistani	27.5	29.7
Bangladeshi	21.7	–

Note: 'Other' categories omitted.
Source: Labour Force Survey, reported in Labour Market Trends (August 1997, p 296)

Table 3: Unemployment rates by ethnicity, gender and qualifications

		No qualification	'O'-level or equivalent	'A'-level or higher
White	Male	10	11	12
	Female	13	10	7
Caribbean	Male	42	31	23
	Female	19	16	16
Indian or	Male	20	20	12
African Asian	Female	13	10	12
Pakistani or	Male	46	36	17
Bangladeshi	Female	54	(42)	(18)

Source: Modood et al (1997, Tables 4.3 and 4.4)

Table 4: Mean weekly earnings of full-time employees

	Men £/w	Women £/w	Mean number in household	% of households having less than half average income
White	336	244	2.4	28
Caribbean	306	267	2.8	41
Indian	287	252	3.9	45
African Asian	335	254	3.9	39
Pakistani	227	(181)	5.1	82
Bangladeshi	191		5.7	84
Chinese	(336)	(287)	3.3	34

Note: household size and percentage below half average income refer to all households, not just those with someone in employment. (Brackets signify an average based on small numbers of cases)

Source: Modood et al (1997, Tables 4.21, 4.22, 2.17 and 5.6)

Table 5: Women's earnings as a percentage of men's (1997)

	Manual	Non-manual	All
Median gross hourly earnings	71	70	83
Mean gross weekly earnings	64	66	73

Source: calculated from New Earnings Survey (1997, Table A1.1)

Table 6: Unemployment by type of location

		Inner London or inner metropolitan	Outer London or outer metropolitan	Rest of England and Wales
White	Male	26	14	12
	Female	12	8	8
Caribbean	Male	41	30	23
	Female	18	18	17
Indian or African Asian	Male	27	15	20
	Female	14	12	11
Pakistani or Bangladeshi	Male	47	40	31
	Female	48	42	31
Percentage of group living in such areas				
White		11	18	71
Caribbean		41	32	27
Indian/African Asian		11	61	29
Pakistani/Bangladeshi		28	42	30

Source: Modood et al (1997, Table 4.7)

Table 7: Tenure by ethnicity, gender and marital status

	Owner-occupation	Social renting	Other renting
White	67	23	9
Caribbean	50	46	4
Indian	85	9	7
African Asian	84	12	7
Pakistani	79	15	6
Bangladeshi	48	45	8
Chinese	54	24	22
Married couples	79	14	8
Single men	51	27	23
Single women	42	38	21
Widowed men	61	35	5
Widowed women	57	36	7
Divorced or separated men	46	36	18
Divorced or separated women	51	39	11
Lone parents	35	54	11
Other families	77	17	7

Source: Modood et al (1997, Table 6.15); ONS (1997, Tables 3.10 and 3.17)

Male exclusion

Increasingly studies are pointing to the issue of male exclusion as a factor in area regeneration (Campbell, 1993; May, 1997; Power and Tunstall, 1997). In many ways this has been sparked by the usual 'problem' focus of policy which places young men at the centre of social unrest on some housing estates (Power and Tunstall, 1997). An appreciation of the gender dimensions of exclusion and poverty is needed to place this in context.

Economic change has led to the decline in areas of work traditionally considered 'male' and an increase in those considered 'women's work'. It is plausible that the lack of a job is more damaging to men than women because of the traditional construction of the man as breadwinner. Women may be able to sustain a sense of worth through competence in juggling a small budget, managing the home and caring for family members. May (1997) notes that men's unwillingness to replace work responsibilities with domestic ones plus their exclusion from work is leading to increasing marginalisation. Paradoxically, Riseborough (1997) suggests that the assumption that women

are doing better than men in the labour market is a further cause of women's concerns about being left off the regeneration agenda.

Campbell (1993) argues that men's and women's experience of and reaction to the situations found on many estates where work has been in scarce supply for generations can be very different. Women respond by working together, either through informal groups or community organisations. Men, especially young men, can respond through anger, crime and violence. There are dangers of setting up stereotypes here and there is a need for further work to explore the dimensions of these issues in more depth. However, it underlines the need to appreciate the diversity of experience of poverty and exclusion.

Implications for regeneration policy and practice

The picture of the differing experiences of living in regeneration areas that even this brief account paints holds within it some major implications for regeneration policy and practice. Firstly, *it is impossible to see these areas as homogenous.* Within any regeneration area there will be different experiences of that area, different needs and different demands across a number of dimensions of which race and gender are two. It follows that accurate baseline information is needed to establish this picture.

Secondly, *just as experience differs, so will routes to regeneration.* For some this may be through work, but to enable this different issues may need to be addressed such as childcare, self-esteem and training. For others, paid work may not be what is needed and economic empowerment through increasing incomes in other ways such as credit unions and energy efficient homes may be more appropriate.

Thirdly, *it is likely that the ways in which regeneration is mediated by relations such as race and gender will be different in each regeneration area.* Generalised accounts such as the one above are no substitute for a detailed understanding of the relationships and dynamics of the local area. *This is why we argue that race and gender awareness must be an essential and integral part of regeneration practice and not something that can be added on as an afterthought.*

Political exclusion and the governance of regeneration

Exclusion and inclusion have political dimensions and again these are mediated by race and gender. Campbell's work quoted above illustrates an issue that is often commented on in the literature but never fully explored, that women typically form the majority of those active on estates. Community organising can be seen as an extension of women's traditional concern with issues outside the world of work, making men reluctant to become involved. It also adds to demands on women. May (1997) notes the 'triple burden' placed on women of work, family and neighbourhood activity. The obverse is the low level of male involvement in community organisations.

Ensuring the involvement of the full range of ethnic groups in regeneration areas can also be difficult. Such areas frequently exhibit not only ethnic mix but also deep tensions across a racialised divide (Hoggett et al, 1994; Harrison

et al, 1995). These tensions may be exacerbated by a competitive bidding process (Loftman and Beazley, 1998). Projects must be aware of these problems but guidance on how to manage this situation is in short supply.

The power of different groups within communities to influence policy at a variety of levels is as important within regeneration as tangible outputs. Membership or control of regeneration agencies operating on a local level is a key factor in this respect, as is the openness of those agencies to influence.

In terms of power and influence at levels above that of the community new forms of governance are emerging, typified by the regeneration partnership. Informal networks are also growing in influence. Research has shown that this emerging system can present barriers to inclusion along the lines of race and gender, but on the other hand may function to offer opportunities for inclusivity. For example, partnerships are not required to follow equal opportunities procedures in terms of membership, informal networks may ignore women's and ethnic minorities' networks while at the same time less bureaucratic ways of working and officer discretion can allow for greater involvement. These issues are explored more fully in the next chapter.

The dynamics of the relationship between partners and between partnerships and other agencies and the community are consequently also mediated by race and gender, for example, if many community representatives are women and other partners are male.

Implications for regeneration policy and practice

Social inclusion is fostered by political inclusion, in other words, by visible evidence that a regeneration project is treating all sections of the community as having the right and the capacity to make a contribution. Projects should encourage all groups in the locality to respect and value each other's cultural traditions and practices. While there must be no exclusions from general purpose local groups, there may also be targeted initiatives catering for particular groups (see below).

The structures and processes of governance have to be looked at carefully for their potential to include or exclude all sections of the community and to nurture different routes to regeneration and empowerment. It is important to build the capacity of organisations to participate and to ensure that these organisations reflect the diversity in areas. But capacity building is also about enabling organisations and the professionals within them to recognise the importance of diversity and to build such a recognition into policy and practice.

Enhancing the physical condition of localities: the spatial dimension

This element of regeneration includes environmental improvements and the development and redevelopment of land and property, particularly for business and housing. It may also include transport and traffic schemes. Although there has been a shift from physical to social regeneration in recent years, improving the physical condition of localities is still high on the regeneration agenda.

As research has shown (Valentine, 1990), experience of the built environment differs for men and women. Women's use of urban space, especially after dark, is structured by fear of violence, which requires constant awareness of which places are likely to be safe at what time. Similar considerations affect the movement of many minority ethnic group members. Personal safety is put at risk as much by sexual and racial hostility as by the design of urban space, but redesign that takes account of community safety can have a significant effect of 'including in' those previously afraid to go out. Safety considerations in planning for transport, location of workplaces and venues for meetings or leisure activities are also important.

Major physical regeneration schemes are likely to have differential impacts for different sections of the community. Improving the environment by, for example, large-scale provision of new private housing, will benefit women and ethnic minorities less than other sections of the community. Different sections of the population are likely to have different needs for facilities such as leisure, public transport and shopping.

Implications for regeneration policy and practice

The built environment is not gender or race neutral. The differential experience of areas needs to be recognised in the planning of physical regeneration schemes. The planning of such schemes must involve widespread consultation and the use of innovative methods such as planning for real. Impact analysis of major schemes should take account of race and gender.

Stimulating the local economy

Regeneration policy is also about promoting local economic development and increasing the competitiveness of areas and cities within an increasingly globalised economy. Many studies note that in areas with minority ethnic populations the opportunities presented by ethnic businesses and employment can be overlooked or undervalued (Oc et al, 1997; Crook, 1995). For example, ethnic restaurants can be seen as cheap fast food rather than as having the potential for investment to move up market and therefore bring in more money to the local economy. In contrast, a number of reports (see, for example, Zahno, 1997) make the point that the global links which ethnic businesses may have can be a vital asset for regeneration.

Further, the issues facing these businesses may be different from those in the mainstream economy. One particular issue identified is the dependence on local customers who may themselves have low incomes. A study carried out by the London Borough of Greenwich (1994) indicated that ethnic minority businesses faced different problems over and above those encountered by white-owned businesses. These included discrimination, racial violence, the reluctance of banks and lending institutions to loan them money, lack of affordable and suitable premises and limited access to council and other major contracts.

Promoting work and training

A growing critique is emerging of the priorities of regeneration which place the emphasis on gaining employment rather than maximising incomes using a variety of means. The Community Development Foundation (CDF) argues that 50% of the population at any one time is unlikely to be working, so initiatives such as credit unions, LETS schemes, energy efficiency or growing food can have more impact on local disposable income.

Again, there is a gender and race dimension to this. As we have seen, increasing household income does not necessarily lead to increased incomes for all the family. However, such policies can be used to recognise different routes out of economic exclusion. For example, the majority of users of high interest loans are women, so creating credit unions in local areas is likely to benefit women. Understanding the complex strategies by which women manage debt and balance low incomes is an important starting point to understanding local economies (May, 1997). LETS schemes, where people exchange services, for example, childcare in return for garden produce, may increase resources, improve the quality of life *and* increase empowerment by valuing people's skills.

Implications for regeneration policy and practice

The implications for regeneration are that ideas of what is considered economic regeneration need to be widened to include all economic activity in the area and strategies such as community businesses and credit unions. There must be a recognition of diverse routes into employment, through training and the differing training needs of women and minority ethnic groups, through building confidence and through the provision of childcare.

Tackling social and community issues

This aspect of regeneration encompasses a wide range of activities including health promotion, community safety, provision of community facilities and the provision of services for a range of groups in the area, such as old people. It is clear that across these issues there will be a diversity of experience and need. We do not propose to elaborate on this aspect as it has traditionally been an area of regeneration activity which has recognised diversity more than most. For example, the Urban Programme in the 1970s supported many black voluntary

organisations and some women's projects. However, there has been a tendency in later regeneration initiatives for diversity issues to be marginalised into this area, rather than incorporated at the strategic and planning stages of programmes.

Implications for regeneration policy and practice

The importance placed on different priorities may well vary for different sections of the local population. A survey in Sandwell, West Midlands, for example, revealed that housing and racial violence topped the list for the minority ethnic population, while for the white population it was jobs and economic development. The challenge to local partnerships is to formulate coherent strategies which articulate these possibly opposing priorities.

Capacity building and sustainable regeneration

While policies and representation are important, so is the way regeneration is carried out. For regeneration professionals to accept the validity of local agendas may be empowering for local people, but can be experienced as disempowering for project workers. They are no longer in control of the process and must live with a high degree of uncertainty. Target setting must have the flexibility to cope with changing priorities. It also requires a particular set of skills and capabilities in regeneration workers as well as residents: perhaps different from those of the 'community entrepreneur' who can make things happen (Thake, 1995) and a long way from the broker of deals for property-led regeneration. 'Community facilitator' would be the most accurate description.

This role too is important in bringing about social as well as political inclusion. Although there may be a need to break through racial hostility or at least stereotyping, there are cases where local groups have eagerly taken up an equal opportunities agenda and have self-managed balanced representation on committees, perhaps more quickly than other participants (Darke and Rowland, 1997). However, there may be quite legitimate demands for separate organisations for some purposes: fatherhood classes, women's fitness classes, Bengali-speaking groups, mentoring for black youngsters, and so on. Depending on the particular locality these may outnumber community-wide initiatives.

Moving on to political inclusion, the first step is to treat local residents and other stakeholders as having the capacity for involvement. At the very least, they will have their own perceptions of the main problems in the locality and what the priorities should be in a regeneration project. Their own realisation that they do indeed possess such expertise is itself empowering. Taylor (1995, p 21) describes how some people resent the term 'capacity building' as implying that they are initially empty vessels, but in fact local knowledge about the issues and potentials in an area is always there, and can be put to use provided only that a project can overcome the legacy of mistrust and political ineffectiveness.

Once the process starts, capacity can be built by using capacities as they develop. Project organisers must ensure that these benefits are reaching many participants rather than being concentrated on the eager few; it is also important to avoid burning out the most active. Again, it may be necessary to give extra support and encouragement to sections of the community that are under-represented.

The increase in the capacities of local people and the growth of organisations may develop in parallel: indeed the latter could be used as an indicator of the former.

Universalism or targeting?

In order to ensure that benefits are reaching all sections of a diverse community, local projects will need a mixture of *universal* initiatives and objectives, and those *targeted* at particular groups.

Universal objectives will be couched with reference to issues such as poverty, social exclusion, low skills, poor health or unemployment. These describe the problems to be tackled without referring to the ethnicity or gender of those experiencing these problems. There are both advantages and drawbacks to objectives being expressed in universal terms.

Phrases such as poverty and social exclusion have become familiar to policy makers in government at local, national and European levels. As a direct measure of need, poverty is preferable to indices that assume that areas of, for example, ethnic minority concentration are bound to be needy. Evidence of problems such as unemployment and ill health will attract funding where this is distributed according to need: a stated aim of the British government and European community policies.

> "We need to move away from talking about race and towards social exclusion. It is impossible within the UK to move on the discussion if we concentrate on race." (Head of equalities in a large local authority)

> "We need a language which is holistic and corporate and does not mention words like race and gender and black at all ... equality should be seen through the prism of social inclusion." (National voluntary organisation representative)

However, such language *may* conceal the fact reiterated many times in this report that women and men and different minority groups experience poverty differently, and need different routes into the mainstream. Even a term such as diversity, used frequently here, can constitute too quick and tokenistic a recognition of different situations.

> "I think we are losing ourselves by thinking we can use nice terms like exclusion and that we're addressing these problems." (Black voluntary organisation representative)

What little research there has been on projects focusing on exclusion indicates that there have been few targeted programmes within them, and these have largely relied on officer-led initiatives and pressure from below.

Where initiatives are designed with and for specific groups, these differences are more likely to call forth an appropriate response. There are benefits for a local area as a whole even when specific groups are targeted. For example, when women or minority ethnic groups articulate their own priorities these often include community safety and the reduction of crime and vandalism. If these priorities are acted upon, the changes will benefit all residents. As noted above, extra resources controlled by women are more likely to be spent in a way that benefits children (May, 1997; Goode et al, 1998).

Making specific targets compulsory, not discretionary, ensures a wider spread of beneficiaries. Some regional offices report that the dialogue entered into with managers and projects over such targets has proved creative in raising awareness and achieving outputs.

However, specifically targeted programmes themselves carry drawbacks. Initiatives that only benefit one ethnic group can reinforce divisions, create resentment and attract the resistance of regeneration professionals. Areas undergoing regeneration are often already characterised by racial tensions and a project should obviously aim to reduce rather than exacerbate them. Furthermore, unless there is good consultation the targeting may be predicated on stereotypes that merely reinforce existing roles: sewing coops for Asian women, recording studios for black youngsters.

Those interviewed for this project held strong but sharply contrasting views on this issue. Local projects must be aware of the problems in each approach and in practice will need both universal and specific initiatives: a strategy we refer to as *twin-tracking*. For example, one of the components of empowerment is confidence-building (Taylor, 1995) and this may be more effective if individuals can initially work with others similar to themselves. However, unless the gains in confidence can be sustained in wider settings their value will be limited.

Conclusions

This brief summary has shown how regeneration issues are mediated by race and gender. Regeneration policies and practices need, therefore, to be informed by an awareness of diversity at all stages of the process: strategy and design, implementation, monitoring and evaluation. Such an approach not only reflects the realities of regeneration areas but has other justifications:

- social justice and equality of opportunities and outcomes;

- ignoring problems does not mean that they go away;

- the uneven spread of benefits of regeneration can be divisive;

- it takes a lead in combating racial segregation and violence;

- the goal of tackling social exclusion and sustainable regeneration is not met otherwise.

In the rest of the report we give examples of where inclusive regeneration is being practised. Before doing so the policy context will be explored, which is the aim of the next chapter.

2

The policy context

If the previous chapter has shown that race and gender are central to regeneration, a review of the literature reveals that race has remained on the margins of policy and practice (Atkinson and Moon, 1994; Thomas et al, 1995; Crook, 1995) while issues of gender have been virtually invisible (May, 1997; Brownill, 1997). Developments within urban policy over the last decade showing a growing concern with social exclusion, partnerships and holistic regeneration not only allow for an end to marginalisation and invisibility but demand it. Nevertheless, reviews of current policy (Crook, 1995; Hall et al, 1996; May, 1997; Loftman and Beazley, 1998; Riseborough, 1997) reveal that barriers to inclusive regeneration remain. Subsequent chapters will look at how such barriers can be overcome. Here the policy context will be set out.

A sense of history

The current policy context cannot be understood without briefly considering the history of race, gender and regeneration policy.

Urban policy

During the 1960s a number of spatially-targeted programmes resulted from the rediscovery of poverty and the appearance of the inner city as a policy issue. From the beginning, an ambiguous relationship with race was apparent. The Urban Programme, for example, was announced two weeks after Enoch Powell's infamous 'rivers of blood speech' yet race was never explicitly mentioned, reflecting the government's fear of being seen to target ethnic minorities (Atkinson and Moon, 1994).

Yet policy was not totally race and gender blind. Instead, it was assumed that poverty could be explained by individual pathology. Thus, women's behaviour such as poor parenting or forming single-parent families, and minority ethnic groups with their perceived failure to assimilate into mainstream society and their threat to law and order, were turned into 'problems' to be addressed. Single parents and the presence of ethnic minorities became labelled as indicators of deprivation but with this labelling went resources. Although the sums were not large, grants to the voluntary sector including black-led and women-led groups brought funding that helped to build capacity which incorporated diversity.

During the late 1970s the policy focus shifted from people to the economy. Starting with the 1977 White Paper on the Inner Cities and subsequent Inner Urban Areas Act this focus on economic forces excluded many of the concerns of women in inner city areas and shifted the focus of funding from revenue to capital, which had a disproportionate effect on minority ethnic groups (Munt, 1994). While racial discrimination was recognised as an element of the inner city problem it was excluded as a specific target of urban policy being left to the Commission for Racial Equality to tackle.

In 1979, with the election of a radical right wing government, urban policy shifted to a belief in the power of the private sector to regenerate the inner city. Thomas et al (1995) note how this ideology was ethnically blind, believing that benefits would trickle down from the largely physical regeneration projects to an undifferentiated local population. The failure of trickle-down to have anything other than a limited impact and for that impact to largely bypass ethnic minorities and women has been well documented (DoE, 1994). Brownill (1993) underlines the implications of ignoring race and gender. Loftman and Beazley (1998) go further:

> The trickle-down effect does not work evenly across disadvantaged communities, therefore black and ethnic minority groups are least likely to benefit. (p 28)

Moreover, the governance of Urban Development Corporations was by centrally-appointed nominees, among whom women and ethnic minorities were hardly represented (Brownill et al, 1996).

Elsewhere the Urban Programme survived, largely in response to serious urban unrest in 1981 and 1985, which was erroneously labelled as 'race riots', but the drift to economic, capital projects persisted. Funding specifically targeted at ethnic minorities such as Section 11 and Ethnic Minority Business Grant achieved a greater level of success in meeting the needs of minority ethnic groups (Oc et al, 1997), although their role in relation to women does not appear to have been researched.

Estate regeneration policy

Through the 1980s policies and practices based on the regeneration of social housing estates were developing. The refurbishment of estates became more thorough and holistic, with resident involvement through localised and responsive housing management. This was supported from the mid-1980s by Estate Action funding from the DoE, allocated by a competitive bidding process. Before this earmarked fund disappeared into the SRB (see below), a degree of expertise on resident involvement had developed, and was the subject of an intensive research effort supported mainly by the Joseph Rowntree Foundation. Yet a review of this research noted that:

> Gender and race are ... given little more than a footnote in the literature on estates. (Stewart and Taylor, 1995, p 72)

The 1990s

Two major initiatives, City Challenge launched in 1991 and the Single Regeneration Budget (SRB) in 1993, have replaced the 1980s emphasis on property-led regeneration and trickle-down with the new buzz words of partnership, competition and holistic regeneration. With the expiry of City Challenge projects in 1998, the SRB has become the central plank in the government's regeneration policy.

Policy in the 1990s has moved towards a greater recognition of *social* regeneration. A concern with the physical transformation of places and economic development has been accompanied by, among other things, an emphasis on poverty and deprivation and community safety. Alongside this has grown the encouragement of the involvement of a wide range of interests in decision making and the implementation of policy. This is enshrined in the priority given to multiagency partnerships as the vehicle for regeneration at the local level. With the short-life nature of many regeneration agencies a further concern has developed around encouraging sustainable regeneration through the building of long-term capacity within areas to carry forward the momentum established.

There are three other significant features of policy in the 1990s. Firstly, it is competitive, with bids assessed against criteria specified by the government. Secondly, the process is target driven, with partners contracted to deliver certain outputs. The achievement or not of targets has probably received greater scrutiny than the appropriateness of the targets selected in the first place. Thirdly, eligibility to bid is not based on need – bids are acceptable from anywhere in the country.

In terms of race and gender, City Challenge bidding guidance stated that plans had to define characteristics and 'problems' of the area which are relevant to the strategy, including the presence of ethnic minority communities (note the use of the word 'problems'). In practice there was no element of compulsion in following this guidance. Neither did core outputs specify targets specific to ethnic minorities. It was therefore left to the discretion of individual City Challenges to take these issues on board. Recent research for the Joseph Rowntree Foundation has found that this resulted in a patchy performance by City Challenges in specifying strategies to benefit and involve minority ethnic communities within their programmes (Oc et al, 1997). Information does not exist on policies towards gender.

The Single Regeneration Budget

According to the bidding guidance issued by government, SRB is:

> ... a catalyst for local regeneration. It complements or attracts other resources – private, public or voluntary. It helps to improve local areas and enhance the quality of life of local people by tackling need, stimulating wealth creation and enhancing competitiveness.... It encourages partners to come together in a strategic approach to meet local needs and priorities. (DETR, 1997a)

Included within the strategic objectives which programmes are required to address is an explicit commitment 'to promote initiatives of benefit to ethnic minorities'. There is no such objective in relation to gender or other aspects of diversity.

These strategic objectives of the SRB are as follows (authors' italics):

1 Enhance the employment prospects, education and skills of local people, particularly the young and *those at a disadvantage*, and promote *equality of opportunity*.

2 Encourage sustainable economic competitiveness of the local economy, including *business support*.

3 Improve housing through physical improvements, greater choice and better management and maintenance.

4 Promote initiatives of *benefit to ethnic minorities*.

5 Tackle crime and *improve community safety*.

6 Protect and improve the environment and infrastructure and promote good design.

7 Enhance the *quality of life* of local people, including their *health* and *cultural* and sports opportunities.

Despite the solitary mention of race and the silence on gender, there are references throughout to issues which call out for disaggregated thinking on how these objectives apply to different groups in the population. We have italicised the more obvious cases. However, projects are only required to meet one or more of the seven strategic objectives, and as we shall see later, in practice, Strategic Objective 4 has received the lowest priority among successful bids.

A further significant feature of the SRB is the fact that it is administered at the regional level by 10 Government Offices for the Regions (GORs) which integrate the activity of several government departments concerned with regeneration. GORs receive and make initial assessments of outline bids and final bids and are encouraged by government to provide a regional strategic framework for regeneration, an aim which has only recently started to be implemented. It is to these regional offices that bids are made and their already significant role is likely to increase with the establishment of Regional Development Agencies in the near future. This devolution to the regional level, plus the fact that the SRB is delivered through local partnerships, means there is scope both for local influence over policy and local variation in policy outcomes.

Monitoring minority ethnic outputs.
SRB is, in reality, a contract between government and a partnership for the delivery of specified outputs. As a result of lobbying from a variety of organisations ethnic monitoring of 'people-oriented' outputs, such as jobs created and educational attainment has been required. Again, there is no such requirement for gender. The focus on the mechanical setting and meeting of targets as the replacement for a process of regeneration has been questioned. However, according to Crook (1995) the inclusion of minority ethnic outputs has:

• enabled an assessment of benefits going to minority ethnic groups;

• allowed negotiations over the setting and meeting of targets;

• provided a vehicle for a broader discussion of equality within the SRB.

Race, gender and the SRB in practice.
Monitoring and the inclusion of a strategic objective on benefiting minority ethnic groups

within the SRB might at first sight appear to indicate that policy has already recognised the relevance of race to the regeneration agenda. However, the reasons for the inclusion of Objective 4 lay less with a change of heart by the DoE than with the insistence by the Home Office that it be included. This is indicative of the fact that the SRB merged 20 previous funding regimes, including the Section 11 grants and other Home Office programmes specifically targeted to help ethnic minorities. In return for placing its funds in the pot, the Home Office asked for this strategic objective. Loftman and Beazley (1998) note that this has led to a reduction in ringfenced resources for ethnic minority groups.

However, initial evaluations of the operation of policy raise questions about the low priority given to the objective, the spread of benefits and the involvement of minority ethnic organisations in all stages of the process (BTEG, 1997; Hall at al, 1996; Loftman and Beazley, 1998). Riseborough (1997) shows that gender is hardly given consideration at all.

Analyses of the first three rounds of the SRB raises a number of questions about the ability of the programme to ensure that race and gender move to the mainstream. Firstly, it appears that few partnerships are prioritising Objective 4 (benefiting ethnic minorities) within their bids. Research by the Centre for Urban and Regional Studies (CURS) has shown that in Round 2 only 2% of local authorities did so, making this the lowest rated strategic objective (Hall et al, 1996). Analysis of Round 3 bids reveals a similar picture, with 65% of respondents identifying ethnic minorities as either their sixth or seventh ranked priority. However, government figures reveal that 37% of successful Round 2 bids are specifically targeted on ethnic minorities and over 60% include specific outputs. As there is no strategic objective for gender, comparable data is not available; however, a survey by Riseborough revealed that less than 10% of local authorities and 12% of TECs included specific references to gender within their bids (Riseborough, 1997).

A review of the projected outputs for minority ethnic groups reveals at first sight substantial potential for benefit. Aggregated figures for ethnic minority benefits in Rounds 1, 2 and 3 indicate (Loftman and Beazley, 1998):

- 52,600 full-time ethnic minority jobs created or safeguarded;
- 14,519 ethnic minority business start-ups;
- 4,676 ethnic minority voluntary/community organisations supported.

However, this conceals some important issues. Firstly, outputs are concentrated within particular regions, particularly London and the West Midlands, where they tend to outstrip the percentage of ethnic minority people in their respective populations. However, Hall et al argue that while outputs exceed the proportion of ethnic minorities in the population, this would only be expected given the fact that ethnic minorities are disproportionately represented in areas of poverty.

Secondly, outputs are concentrated in a few large bids. For example, in Round 2 five bids accounted for 71% of ethnic minority school pupils benefiting, 62% of ethnic minority jobs safeguarded and 49% of ethnic minority jobs created (Hall et al, 1996). Once again there are no figures available for benefits by gender.

Partnerships, networks and inclusion and exclusion

Most of the literature reviewed notes the rise of partnerships between the public, private, voluntary and community sectors in policy making and implementation in urban regeneration. Alongside partnerships the importance of informal networks has been increasingly noted (Skelcher et al, 1996). Networks can be defined as informal connections linking some or all of the variety of agencies and interests involved in regeneration (Skelcher et al, 1996). While they do not have the same decision making and implementation role as partnerships, networks can become formalised into partnerships. Networks also have an important role in influencing local and regional policy and sharing information and good practice at a variety of levels.

The growth in partnerships and networks in urban regeneration and other areas of policy is one example of the emergence of a new system of urban governance as opposed to directly elected local government. While relatively few studies address the impact of this emerging system on inclusion and exclusion (Brownill et al, 1996; BTEG, 1995; Riseborough, 1997; Geddes, 1997; Skelcher et al, 1996) the evidence that does exist suggests that partnerships represent a contradictory potential for inclusivity. Their structures and working practices can both include and exclude. It is therefore important to acknowledge the barriers to inclusion and work to overcome them.

In doing so it is important to distinguish between the *structures* of partnerships, that is, their membership, and the *processes* or the way of working which they adopt. Partnership working can bring with it a particular approach to achieving aims and objectives, and represents a particular way in which power and decision making operates, both of which may have a bearing on inclusivity. The rest of this chapter addresses this issue looking firstly at partnership structure and secondly at styles of governance.

Silent partners?

What is the evidence in terms of inclusion and exclusion in partnerships? The little information available reveals some interesting trends. In terms of minority ethnic groups the London Boroughs Grants Unit (LBGU) has shown that 23% of bids involved minority ethnic partners in Round 3 of the SRB, up from 15% in Round 1 (LBGU, 1997). This may underestimate minority ethnic involvement as members may be added as co-optees or from sub-groups of the partnership.

A survey by the London Regeneration Network (LRN) revealed that under 35% of partnership board members were women (LRN, 1997). This may appear low but it is better than, for example, the figures for women's involvement on Urban Development Corporation boards (Brownill, 1997). This showed that throughout the lifetime of the London Docklands Development Corporation there was at most one woman board member at any one time.

In the West Midlands a study showed that 25% of local authority-led and 32% of TEC-led partnerships involved women's groups. In addition, few respondents indicated that any specific attention was paid to attract women partners or to reflect women's concerns in partnerships. The West Midlands survey showed a better picture in respect of ethnic minorities, with 43% of local authorities and 58% of TECs indicating minority ethnic involvement in partnerships; however, the level of involvement was not specified (Riseborough, 1997).

It is important to note that partnerships can change during their lifetime. Experience in the West Midlands indicates that while minority ethnic groups may have been missing at the outset, through pressure from minority ethnic organisations and the voluntary sector in general, representation on the boards of six partnerships studied by BTEG was achieved over time (Crook, 1995).

There are some interesting though contradictory findings on which sector women and minority ethnic representatives are coming from. Geddes (1997) showed that where women are on partnerships they are more likely to come from the community sector. This is contradicted by Riseborough's survey (1997) which showed the private sector as the greatest source of women representatives. Both could be seen as a reflection of the fact that the 'community' is seen as a woman's place and that mixed organisations choose women to represent them at this level. We have not been able to locate any comparable figures for minority ethnic representatives.

These figures may appear encouraging but it is a sobering thought that in the first three rounds of the SRB, out of 555 successful bids, only four were led by minority ethnic organisations (Loftman and Beazley, 1998). Figures for women's organisations are not even collected.

Furthermore, caution is needed in interpreting these figures. Firstly, there is no necessary requirement for women or for ethnic minority representatives to reflect women's or ethnic minority views. They may be there as representatives of a council or a private firm. Secondly, there is no guarantee that a seat at the table will be translated into power. The question of equality between partners is returned to later.

Factors in exclusion include:

- timescales of bid preparation are too short to allow meaningful consultation;

- many organisations do not have the capacity, information, or regeneration expertise to participate fully, particularly as lead or key partners;

- the concentration on strategic issues excludes many organisations concerned with race and gender who often concentrate on local level welfare and social provision.

Key funding programmes such as City Challenge and the SRB have included few structural safeguards on representation. Partly because of this, some partnerships exhibit a passive rather than a pro-active attitude to gender and race equality issues. (Geddes, 1987, p 110)

It all depends on who you know

Partnerships and networks are often formed on the basis of whether organisations and their representatives are known by and visible to those initiating them. Work by Skelcher et al (1996) on networks indicates that there are barriers to inclusion along the lines of race and gender. This is illustrated in the words of their informants:

> "Black networks are very much there ... but operate quite possibly on a different basis. If they don't conform to the LA view then they [the agencies] are not going to see them and they are going to lose out."

> "... women's networks are organic ... often invisible in the workplace and, if recognised, seen as threatening or trivialised."

> "... in the voluntary sector there are a clique of people who get access to funds ... black organisations are on the outside because the networks say 'we are dubious about working with them'."

These informal networks may therefore act as yet another hurdle for women and black organisations, while for others in the voluntary sector they may be leading to access to resources and power.

Unequal partners

Many reviews of partnerships note that the rhetoric hides a reality in which some partners, notably, local authorities and Training and Enterprise Councils (TECs), dominate (Hastings et al, 1996; Skelcher et al, 1996). This is in part a structural issue (partnerships have to have lead partners for administrative purposes) but is related to the resources available to each partner. It is also linked to partnership processes which are examined next.

Ways of working in partnerships: men in suits make me fall silent

Partnerships are not just about structures and representation – although this is important. They are also about particular ways of working and decision making which have an impact in inclusion and exclusion. Furthermore, each partner brings to the table different assumptions about other partners and different styles of power.

Here are aspects about partnerships as a style of governance which have an impact on issues of diversity.

Speed of operation: tight bidding timetables and short-life agencies mean that speed is often of the essence. The perception, and indeed the fact that consultation is time-consuming means short-cuts are often taken which can exclude organisations outside the usual networks.

Output driven: partnerships are concerned about meeting the targets that have been set in terms of output and performance and this can narrow the range of concerns they take on.

The 'can-do' culture: the need for speed and to meet targets can often promote a culture within organisations of being focused and getting on with the job. Agencies have different structures of officer accountability, often leading to high levels of discretion. The checks and balances of equal opportunities are often not a part of these agencies.

Different cultures: partnerships bring together partners with a range of different cultures. They may hold assumptions about other partners and each partner can have a different way of working. Loftman and Beazley (1998) have found a lack of trust and understanding between partners, and particularly between ethnic minority groups and local authorities, to be a major barrier to inclusive partnerships.

What has been referred to as styles of power (Gilroy, 1996) can have an impact on inclusion, as the following quote shows:

> "When I go [to board meetings] there is something about men in suits which makes me fall silent. I feel I can't speak because who will back me up, will *they* [the men in suits] agree or just *put* me down." (Woman community representative, quoted in Gilroy, 1996)

Others consider that "the private sector runs a mile from equal opportunities" (woman's organisation representative).

In the following chapter we look at initiatives which have sought to break down these barriers.

Related and future policy directions

Urban policy is at yet another cross-roads. A change in government has strengthened some of the trends outlined above, with emphasis on social need and the aim of achieving a more equal society. The area focus of the SRB is complemented by national programmes, such as Welfare to Work and the Social Exclusion Unit. Future policy looks set to confirm these trends with a recent consultation paper including one of the few government definitions of regeneration as "tackling local needs and priorities associated with poverty and deprivation." (DETR, 1997d). The argument is no longer that social regeneration is needed in order to ensure that physical regeneration is sustainable: rather, regeneration *is* social regeneration.

The openings suggested by these initiatives mean that there is all the more reason to promote strategies for inclusive regeneration. History shows that this is vital if the past marginalisation of some groups is not to repeat itself in the future.

3

From the margins to the mainstream: vision, strategy and partnership in inclusive regeneration

Issues of race and gender are central to an understanding of regeneration, yet they are often invisible or at the margins of policy and practice. This section of the report examines the experience of initiatives and approaches which are working to place race and gender in the mainstream of regeneration to establish the benefits, success factors and barriers to achieving this aim.

In the course of this review a variety of entry points to promoting inclusivity have been found. This reflects the view that came strongly from many of the contributors to this research, that there can be no one blueprint for putting race and gender at the centre of regeneration. May (1997), for example, concludes that in promoting gender awareness a combination of approaches is needed.

As such it is possible to identify four main areas where intervention and initiatives are both effective and necessary: strategy and vision, partnership and governance, implementation and monitoring, and evaluation and research. These will be looked at in turn over this and the next chapter.

Strategy and vision

Chapter 1 showed that regeneration policies are unlikely to address the causes of the factors they are seeking to tackle unless race and gender are recognised as *strategic issues* cross-cutting all areas of policy and practice. Intervention in the area of strategy is therefore a vital first stage to promoting greater inclusivity.

The evidence suggests that *strategic intervention to promote race and gender aware approaches is important at a variety of levels, national, regional and local.* A 'top-down' strategic intervention needs to be complemented by a 'bottom-up' perspective, which recognises the importance of diverse routes to regeneration and empowerment.

Studies show that an important success factor in getting race and gender on the strategic agenda is *involvement in and influence over the partnerships and networks* which have been shown to be so key within current regeneration policy and practice. Therefore, issues around the governance of policy need to be considered at the strategic level. Finally, the *process* of strategic planning is important as an area of inclusivity in its own right.

In the rest of this chapter examples are given of a variety of levels of strategic intervention which are placing issues of diversity centre stage and the lessons and implications of these are drawn out.

The national and regional policy framework

Strategic intervention at the national and increasingly the regional level has been shown to be an important point of intervention in promoting the visibility of race and gender in regeneration policy and practice.

Despite the limitations identified in national policy in Chapter 2, the inclusion of a specific strategic objective for benefiting ethnic minorities has had an impact, as the contrast with gender where there is no such objective shows. The placing of race on the national agenda for the SRB was a result of pressure from the Home Office, a national government department. Many of those interviewed as part of this research commented that a similar lead from the DETR was necessary to ensure the resulting strategic objective was fully implemented. The inclusion of objectives relating to gender and similar pressure from the top to implement it was also identified for action. May (1997) reveals that departments responsible for regeneration policy, in the main, have not prioritised gender as an issue. She cites examples in the Overseas Development Agency and Department for Employment and Education (DfEE) whose proactive stances are taken as examples of good practice.

With the creation of GORs and Regional Development Agencies intervention at the regional level is becoming increasingly important to regeneration policy. Loftman and Beazley (1998) show that the role of the regional offices, and in particular, the Home Office secondee within them, has proved to be critical in promoting inclusivity in respect of ethnic minorities and the SRB. However, in the absence of specific DETR guidance, this has been variable with some GORs active in placing demands on lead partners to include ethnic minorities and specify minority ethnic outputs and others being less so.

GORs are required to draw up regional SRB frameworks. It is possible but again not mandatory for these to include reference to ethnic minorities and gender at the strategic level. For example, the regional framework statement of the West Midlands Government Office states:

> English remains the second language within some communities presenting challenges in the education system and the workplace. Regrettably racial discrimination is perceived to be an obstacle to success for many of these communities. It is important that the SRB backs schemes which help these groups to share better in the prosperity of the region. *Bids which directly involve ethnic minority communities as partners in the planning and delivery of initiatives will be particularly welcome.* (Loftman and Beazley, 1998, p 52; their emphasis)

Initiatives at the local level

While national and regional activity sets the framework, it is at the local level that most regeneration activity takes place. A number of approaches can be identified which have sought to recognise diversity through creating different routes to regeneration.

Placing race and gender at the core of regeneration.
The following case studies show how race and gender awareness can drive policy at the strategic level.

Rich Mix: valuing diversity

The words Rich Mix represent an idea whose time has come. Every city, every region, every nation is a blend of cultures, peoples and communities and that blend will become more intense as time goes on. We can face this with fear or open-mindedness. We can retreat into our shell or acknowledge it with a sure touch. We can communicate or be in conflict. The time is right for an era of inclusiveness, tolerance and empathy, because by mixing we can unleash untold energies. (London Borough of Tower Hamlets, nd)

Rich Mix, a project linked to Cityside SRB in Tower Hamlets, has sought to place ethnic minorities at the core of London's role as a global city. Not only do minority ethnic businesses often have transnational links but cities in the future will increasingly attract residents and visitors from around the world. Its starting point is that London's multicultural diversity is a major asset and that intercultural understanding is a need, opportunity and worthwhile promise.

The proposal is for a 'flagship' national centre to house: a museum of the contribution of immigrants to the culture and economy of the area and to London's role as a world city; exhibition spaces; a market centre for food and artifacts from different cultures; audio-visual recording and performing facilities; and a genealogical centre which will enable visitors to trace their roots and a library. The proposed location of the centre in Spitalfields, which has a long history of being a gateway to a variety of ethnic groups, is symbolic of what the project is trying to achieve.

The concept for the Centre has taken 10 years to develop and has not been without problems. For example, the funding application to the Millennium Commission which formed the background to this case study was unsuccessful. Holding together the alliance of minority ethnic groups, other organisations in the area and the private sector has not proved easy (Eade, 1998). However, the potential benefits of such an approach can be contrasted with the 'global city' developments just down the road in Docklands, where large-scale regeneration has exacerbated racial tension in the area and failed to benefit the minority ethnic population (Brownill, 1993).

An inclusive city vision

The 'Coventry Community Plan' was drawn up by the City Council to set out a vision for the city and a five-year programme to address the city's needs. The plan was drawn up after widespread consultation with and involvement of various stakeholders in the city and is signed by 36 partners, including the Coventry Race Equality Council, local businesses, colleges and voluntary organisations.

The plan has an overall objective "to make measurable improvements by 2003 in economic, social and physical conditions in Coventry" and has six priority areas: jobs, crime, poverty, young people, the city centre and older people. An underlying principle for the whole plan is the recognition that: "Coventry is a multicultural, diverse community in which all organisations commit themselves to equality of opportunity and social justice for everyone. This means we will:

• engage all sections of society;
• combat racism;
• improve access for people with disabilities;
• celebrate diversity of culture."

While it is noticeable that this statement makes no direct reference to gender it is reflected in the inclusion under each of the priority headings of specific actions aimed at diversity. For example, under the jobs priority barriers to employment will be tackled through dealing with discrimination, providing childcare and campaigning for unemployment data to include ethnic origin (Coventry City Council, 1998). The plan shows that a mix of universal aims and specific principles and targets can be effectively combined into an inclusive vision.

Tapping new strengths, adding new value.
A number of other initiatives have taken the same route as Rich Mix and sought to use their diversity in pursuit of a regeneration strategy which:

> ... seeks to build on the uniqueness and distinctiveness of an area, tapping its strengths and finding new opportunities so that it is able to be competitive.
> (Zahno, 1997, p 2)

Oc et al's (1997) analysis of City Challenge vision statements shows how minority ethnic groups and ethnic businesses can be a major resource within regeneration areas, adding value to the local economy. Green Street SRB in the London Borough of Newham, for example, has developed its local economy, which is dominated by ethnic businesses, by promoting the area as a sub-regional shopping centre for London's Asian population. Strategies for promotion include advertising on Asian cable TV channels, thus breaking out of the dependency on the local population for economic support.

The benefits of recognising the potential and realising the value within diverse localities can be seen in a much improved local economy. Yet the ability of such a strategy to benefit minority ethnic women needs to be considered. Although the economic development of Green Street has been a success, a domestic violence project targeted at Asian women has had a more turbulent existence.

An example where recognising the gender dimensions to tackling poverty and exclusion has been successful is provided by the Brownlow Community Trust.

Recognising how social exclusion affects women: the Brownlow Community Trust

Brownlow is a housing estate 25 miles from Belfast, isolated and without economic and social infrastructure. The Brownlow Community Trust was formed in the 1960s and is made up of statutory and community representatives, including several women. The Trust secured funding under the EU Poverty 3 Programme from 1989 to 1994. Their strategy prioritised three groups: women, children and the unemployed.

The decision to target women reflected a recognition of the fact that women tended to carry many of the burdens of poverty and deprivation and that they were discriminated against in gaining jobs through poor childcare, lack of training and poor public transport.

A number of projects were initiated which included: a women's centre (managed by local women and providing a meeting space), training courses and a creche; a young mothers' group, which met regularly and started a programme of classes in personal development; an Asian women's group, which had an Asian lay health worker attached to it; training in a range of skills; and a non-traditional skills project which has sought to promote opportunities for young women to work in areas not traditionally thought of as 'women's jobs'. In addition, a women's forum was formed with representation on the Brownlow Community Trust and a number of women's project officers employed.

Geddes (1997), in evaluating this project, notes how it was successful in maintaining the momentum after EC funding ended because of the active support and involvement of local women.

Using existing strategic objectives.
While there is no strategic objective within the SRB that relates directly to gender, a number of examples exist where the objectives that do exist can be used to promote initiatives which do. For example, the Women's Design Service is working with groups of Asian women in the King's Cross area on growing food in cities. It may not have the output of creating jobs but there are a number of other priorities which are met:

- improving health through a healthier diet;

- using skills that women may have brought from rural areas in their countries of origin;

- increasing disposable income through cutting food bills;

- enabling women to meet together.

This initiative values the contribution that women make to the wealth of local areas.

The community safety objective of the SRB has also proved to be an effective entry point for addressing issues of race and gender. Projects tackling racial harassment on estates, for example the Silwood Estate in Lewisham, have been promoted.

Riseborough (1997) refers to a Safe Estates for Women initiative formed by local women on an estate which had been the focus of numerous regeneration initiatives in the past, with the aim of improving the safety for women and children on the estate. They carried out a safety audit and learnt survey techniques and interviewing skills so they could carry out a survey of women's top priorities. Not only did this benefit the women but the safer crossings, better lighting and safer underpasses benefited all on the estate, including the businesses, showing that specific initiatives can have universal benefits.

Recognising diverse routes to regeneration.
Top-down strategies need to be complemented by an approach which recognises the diversity of routes to regeneration. Such an example is provided by the case study of Cruddas Park in Newcastle.

Cruddas Park: different routes to empowerment

This initiative noted that there were different routes to empowerment: through accessing jobs, through increasing self-confidence and through acting together and influencing policy. These routes were often gender differentiated:

> While many men were taking the route to jobs, many women (and some men) were taking another individualised route ... to self esteem. (Gilroy, 1996, p 253)

Thus, while one strand of activity was looking at ways to get people into work through training, community businesses and seeking job pledges from local employers, another strand based around the nursery school was looking at self-development. Through the headteacher opening the school for the use of parents a women's group was started and then an adult literacy group. For some this was a step to employment; for others the group itself was enough:

> "I got the mothers together and took on this role really with a lot of encouragement from the head. It was the first time in my life someone took an interest in me and hadn't disregarded me – I had some value to give." (quoted in Gilroy, 1996, p 254)

Yet it is well to remember the limitations in terms of the numbers of people such an approach can benefit. Many projects will proudly point to one or two people who have achieved benefit from a project; however, this could be a drop in the ocean compared to overall levels of need. Another writer on regeneration in Newcastle has drawn attention to the reluctance of men to get involved in a community initiative, apart from a small group who were gay (McCulloch, 1997).

Other diverse routes.
Oc et al's (1997) detailed study of ethnic minority training and business advice in City Challenge areas provides examples of the different needs of ethnic minorities in relation to training and enterprise support. Importantly, it also points out the very different requirements of ethnic minority women. Because Asian women are particularly poorly represented in power structures, provision for this group has often been based on stereotypes rather than consultation and empowerment.

These examples show how a flexible strategy which recognises that routes to regeneration may well be gendered and mediated by race can unleash potential at an individual and a community-wide level.

Strategic thinking at the level of the community

One of the challenges presented by current regeneration policy is the need for women's and minority ethnic communities and voluntary organisations to engage at the strategic level. Crook (1995) and Zahno (1997) point out that this calls for organisations to think beyond immediate concerns, for example, service provision, to the way in which this activity can fit into a broader strategy for the area. This entails building alliances and networks as well as developing a vision and strategy. Specialist regeneration agencies, such as BTEG and the Women's Design Service, have proved that they can play a valuable role in developing such a strategic vision.

Experience has shown that such a vision is important in enabling regeneration professionals and agencies to see the value of inclusivity:

> "They have to understand what your vision is as a network and a programme.... What you're trying to achieve. We're trying to maximise their objectives. We're here to say how we can move forward effectively in a way relevant to government and us. Once they appreciate that they are prepared to work with you." (Representative of BTEG)

Zahno articulates a vision for the black voluntary sector:

> The Black Voluntary Sector of the future would consist of networking and support organisations at every level who would elect partners to local regeneration boards, thus influencing, and actually becoming, key decision makers.... The role of the umbrella groups would be to campaign, consult and exert real influence.... There would be two or three regeneration agencies operating at a local authority level, delivering a number of linked regeneration services. Campaigning and advocacy groups at regional and national level would get more involved in campaigning around regeneration issues. Umbrella organisations would support service deliverers and social/informal groups to become more active in regeneration and thus to become more effective as organisations. (Zahno, 1997, p 13)

The process of strategic planning.
The ways in which strategies are drawn up can be as important as the objectives they contain. Many studies argue for extensive consultation in strategic planning and for the use of techniques such as community profiling which build up accurate pictures of local areas. These are returned to in more detail in Chapter 4. An equal opportunities checklist for ensuring racial equality in SRB bids is included in Appendix A.

Strategic partnerships and networks

> "Partnership is the integral element of the programme, which means involvement in partnerships is mainstreaming as far as I'm concerned." (Black voluntary sector representative)

The importance of partnerships to the successful promotion of inclusive strategies cannot be underestimated. Many regeneration partnerships have dual roles, as agencies of decision making and delivery mechanisms for regeneration projects. These will be examined in turn.

Partnerships as agencies of governance

Government has belatedly recognised the value of structural safeguards to inclusivity. The Round 4 SRB bidding guidance states:

> ... partnerships must include other relevant interests ... including ethnic minority and faith communities. (DETR, 1997a)

However, gender is not a consideration and 'good practice' advice in the form of the government's guide to effective partnerships (DoE, 1997b) makes no mention of involving women and minority ethnic groups within its otherwise detailed recommendations.

There exist a number of ways in which partnerships have been successfully seeking to widen involvement and promote equal opportunities, for example:

- entering into concordats with local Race Equality Councils of other organisations to ensure independent monitoring not only of membership but of all aspects of the partnership;

- lead partners adopting policies to ensure race and gender are engaged with throughout the regeneration process (see Appendix A on Haringey);

- seeing partnerships as a process and seeking to widen involvement over time by co-opting members;

- GOR monitoring of partnerships has also been useful.

There are arguments for and against the setting of equalities requirements for partnership membership. The arguments *against* are that it would lead to mechanistic and tokenistic representation and the undervaluing of the representatives that result.

> "I'm sick of being asked to sit on partnership boards as 'the voice of the black community'. It's just such a token gesture." (quoted in McCabe et al, 1997)

One way to counter this is to appoint representatives according to their skills and contributions and not just their race or gender (Crook, 1995). Linking representation to active networks can also undermine accusations of unrepresentativeness. For example, in Coventry an Ethnic Minority Development Alliance was formed by ethnic minority organisations with an interest in regeneration issues.

Resentment at and resistance to an element of compulsion may also result. For example, the reserving of places for Afro-Caribbean representatives in the Toxteth Granby partnership in Liverpool led to negative reaction from white organisations (Geddes, 1997).

Arguments *for* reserved places state that the benefits that result from inclusion outweigh any disadvantages associated with targets. Guidelines would assist those who are working towards greater inclusion to meet their aims. Evidence from GORs which have required additions to membership shows that the ensuing dialogue has been positive and has strengthened the partnership process as a result. It is important that any requirements are seen as part of a process and not as an end in themselves.

Reserving places for representatives, adopting an equal opportunities policy

The Greenwich Waterfront Partnership specifies that one member from its community forum and one from its business forum should be from an ethnic minority. It has also adopted a Partnership Equal Opportunities Statement:

> The Greenwich Waterfront Development Partnership is committed to ensuring the principle of equal opportunities underlies its support of regeneration activities. The partnership believes that the human resources, talents and skills available throughout the Waterfront community can contribute to the regeneration of the area. It looks to individual partners to reflect this commitment in their programmes of activity.

Lead and key partners: partnerships as delivery mechanisms

Lead or key partners in the SRB are those responsible for delivering the agreed outputs. This status is important as it represents a greater degree of power and influence, access to resources and control over who is likely to benefit from such resources. The previous chapter noted some of the barriers within the present system to the involvement of organisations concerned with race and gender. The case study examples show how these can be overcome.

Process in partnerships and networks: building awareness and capacity

The West Midlands case study indicates the importance of *capacity building* to ensure a more even playing field within the regeneration game. The West Midlands bid is an example of a targeted capacity building programme. An example of a universal bid which targeted women and ethnic minorities is provided by the Sandwell case study. However, Loftman and Beazley (1998) make the important point that capacity building should be carried out by the sector itself rather than being top-down.

Key partner: Blackbird Leys, Round 1 SRB, Oxford

This bid was successful in Round 1 of the SRB. The City Council, which was involved in drawing up the bids, asked for projects to be submitted from a number of organisations within its network. Ethnic Minority Business Service and the Women's Training Centre were two such organisations. Oxford City Council was keen to put projects relating to race and gender in the first round bid as it was assumed they would be factors in deciding successful bids. The organisations have found the bureaucracy associated with SRB onerous and the County Council has provided support. In later rounds these groups were not invited to bid as Oxford City Council realised the regional office were not prioritising race and gender. This case study shows the importance of a proactive lead partner, the need for administrative support and the need for GOR direction.

Lead bidder: West Midlands Black Voluntary Sector Regional Regeneration Network

West Midlands regional capacity building

This bid is for a regional regeneration network in the West Midlands. It covers six local authority areas and has the following aims:

- to strengthen local black organisations, communities and networks, and to increase interaction between regeneration agencies and the black voluntary sector;

- to attract additional resources into the region, and in particular, to black voluntary organisations, by influencing regional and sub-regional policy and spending programmes; to promote community ownership and sustainability in the regeneration process.

The network promises to deliver support services to black organisations including training and capacity building to develop organisational capacity, improving communications in the region and promoting networking, acting as an advocate and improving communication with policy makers, and providing funding advice and training in the writing and managing of bids.

The starting point for the bid was research into the exclusion of ethnic minority organisations from the SRB. The bid emerged over a number of years through the activity of voluntary and community organisations, a growing regional network of ethnic minority organisations and the encouragement of the GOR. Problems were encountered both in responding to the onerous requirements for the administration of the SRB, which have slowed down the meeting of initial targets, and in the negative response of some key players in the region who opposed the bid.

It is important to stress that capacity building is not just about developing skills and expertise among women's and ethnic minority organisations. As Zahno (1997) states:

> ... capacity building is more than strengthening and making an organisation effective internally. It is about enabling the [organisations] to have a real influence over how decisions are taken which effect black communities. (Zahno, 1997, p 15)

Thus, enabling a greater range of organisations to participate means addressing the capacities of other partners to work with them.

Structural safeguards are important in promoting inclusivity, but as the previous chapter showed, the ways in which partnerships operate can also restrict involvement. Styles of power, which are themselves gendered and racialised, can entrench the inherent inequalities within partnerships.

Skelcher at al (1996) note how an understanding of respect for the different culture of participants, a common language and internal ground rules are important in breaking down barriers in the ways in which partnerships operate. An example of a training exercise which aims to promote such an understanding is given in Appendix C.

May (1997) draws on Oxfam's experience in the South to show that capacity building is also about increasing the capacity of existing regeneration agencies and professionals to take on board and promote inclusive regeneration. Proven methods to achieve this include:

- working with staff to challenge assumptions through training sessions;
- the use of specialist staff;
- tools and training materials.

Factors for success

Various factors for success in promoting inclusive strategies and partnerships can be identified from the case studies and examples given in this chapter. These include the following:

Recognising that race and gender are strategic regeneration issues: examples such as Rich Mix and the Brownlow Community Trust show the effectiveness and benefits of recognising race

---

Sandwell capacity building

Sandwell Borough Council in the West Midlands secured funds from SRB Round 2 for a community capacity building programme. Four broad areas for development were selected: organisational capacity (building networks and access to decision making) community capacity (developing the potential of voluntary, community and ethnic minority organisations); business capacity (improving links between the business sector and the community sector); evaluation and monitoring. Organisational capacity and benefiting ethnic minorities were given top priority within this.

The programme is made up of 48 different projects. These were selected through a Capacity Building Theme Group of 12 members, half of which had to be from the voluntary and community sectors. The Theme Group is also the main delivery mechanism for the programme with responsibility for monitoring.

Under organisational capacity, projects include the setting up of a Sandwell women's forum and a Sandwell ethnic minority forum to fill identified gaps in the local infrastructure and to provide effective voices within regeneration for these groups within regeneration. Building Business Capacity includes training for ethnic minority people. Community Capacity programmes include a project specifically aimed at young ethnic minority people to promote "increased self-esteem within disadvantaged groups leading to increased involvement in the regeneration and decision-making process, particularly targeted at young people and women" (LGIU, 1997, Appendix).

and gender as factors behind regeneration issues such as poverty and economic development.

Proactive intervention by GORs and lead partners: the role of GORs and in particular the Home Office secondee within them has been shown to be a key factor in promoting greater engagement with diversity. Ways in which GORs have been proactive include: the widespread dissemination of information; organising seminars on inclusivity and the bidding process; ensuring minority ethnic outputs are included in delivery plans; and monitoring membership of partnerships. At a local level a similar role has been played by some lead partners.

Local and regional networks: an effective network at the regional and local level which involves organisations specialising in race and gender issues is important. Similarly, as an effective platform for influencing policy and to build capacity, specific networks for minority ethnic organisations and women's organisations are crucial. These can assist in meeting the challenge to such groups of working on the strategic level.

Processes in partnerships: recognising and valuing what each partner brings is important for creating a shared vision about the aims of partnerships (Wilson and Charlton, 1997). Real capacity building comes from breaking out of traditional ways of working to allow for the building of trust and respect.

Support from umbrella organisations: the role of specialist umbrella and regeneration agencies has been shown to be important in promoting inclusion in partnerships and strategy. Adequate levels of resources for these organisations need to be secured.

Coping with the bureaucracy: ways around this have included:

- mentoring: an established organisation works with a small organisation to submit a bid and to build up the organisational capacity required for administering it;

- support from GORs who have helped bidders through the process;

- a proactive stance on the part of the lead partner.

Building on strengths, not seeing weaknesses: the view held of black and minority ethnic organisations in particular, but also of women's organisations and the voluntary sector in general, is that of a poorly coordinated and poorly resourced sector. A three-stage process is needed to challenge this. One is that funders and policy makers challenge their assumptions and see the opportunities in working with such organisations. Secondly, voluntary organisations need to work together to raise the profile of their sectors and finally, resourcing and capacity building is needed to build effective networks.

Perseverance: many of these initiatives have taken many years to evolve and have encountered significant difficulties along the way.

Building success through strategic intervention: capacity building: building the capacity of all organisations in the regeneration arena is a vital step to success. Strategic intervention to build this capacity has been shown to be effective in leading to more involvement and to raising awareness of the need for and benefits of inclusive regeneration.

We have given examples of a range of initiatives that have incorporated issues of race and gender in their visions for regenerating their area and in the strategic partnerships that have been formed around these. In the following chapter we look at how race and gender can be brought to the mainstream in terms of the implementation of regeneration policy.

4

Implementing inclusive regeneration

Strategies and partnerships provide a basis for mainstreaming, but regeneration is not just a concept but a process. The level of implementation is therefore a vital entry point for greater inclusivity. This chapter looks at various examples of how the process of implementation can be part of the overall aim of recognising diversity in regeneration. Such a process includes drawing up a profile of an area, setting targets and outputs and monitoring them and ensuring effective consultation with all sections of the community. A proven range of tools exist to assist this process.

Know your area: mapping and baseline information

An inclusive strategy needs to start from a sound knowledge of a local area. It is vital that this information is disaggregated by gender and by ethnicity to reflect the fact, as shown in Chapter 1, that the experience of poverty, unemployment and living in an area varies between different groups.

Such information should include the following:

- the ethnic make up of the population;
- family types and structure, including households headed by women;
- labour force participation, wage levels and unemployment for white and minority ethnic men and women;
- households claiming benefit by gender and ethnicity of household head;
- incidence of racial attacks or violence;

- educational attainment of white and minority ethnic boys and girls;
- intra-household dynamics.

Profiles need to reflect the dynamics of gender and race within localities. In some regeneration areas competition between different groups for outputs and racial tensions and attacks may predominate. In others there may be more of a shared identity around a sense of place which transcends such divisions or allows different groups to work together. Obviously this will have an impact on what kind of strategies are needed and are feasible.

In addition, a profile of the organisational capacity of the locality is needed to identify the extent to which all sections of the community and voluntary sectors are involved and the extent of influence over decision making. The following checklist provides a blueprint.

Profile of community activity and the local community and voluntary sector

- What community groups and voluntary organisations are functioning in the locality?
- How many groups are minority ethnic-led or women-led?
- What issues are they concerned with?
- What are their activities?
- What are their catchment areas?
- Which residents do they serve and how many of them?
- What is their potential for expansion and

increased effectiveness?

- How do they involve the most disadvantaged people?

- What obstacles do they face?

- How far do they network and cooperate?

- How well are they supported by umbrella bodies and development projects?

- Are there effective channels for representing their views in the regeneration scheme?

- What is the composition of their membership?

- Who is on their management committees? (Adapted from CDF, 1997)

The gathering of this information is likely to be an on-going process rather than being completed at the outset. As well as providing invaluable information, such profiles are essential in providing baseline information for monitoring and assisting in the drawing up of action plans and targets.

There are a variety of ways in which baseline information can be collected.

- Official statistics such as the Census, employment and crime information and other published sources. Some authorities such as Leeds and Coventry are developing innovative computer systems to collate information on a city-wide level which can be made available to programmes and partnerships.

- Information on local services and service delivery provided by service providers.

- Household and other surveys.

Such sources must be supplemented by other methods which enable residents to define the problems for themselves and to ensure that those often excluded from consultation are included. This will allow the project access to local opinion on priorities, will itself contribute to capacity building and will give participants a sense of ownership of the project. Methods that have been successful in this respect are given below. While important in gathering information, these techniques can also be used in other aspects of the implementation, particularly consultation.

- Involving women's and minority ethnic organisations in collecting information. This happened with the Hopscotch Asian Women's Centre (see example below).

- A similar method that is transferable from the South is participatory rapid appraisal (PRA) (May, 1997). PRA was developed as a way of facilitating local groups targeted for development projects in the South to define their own needs and communicate them to development aid workers. It involves working with a small team of local people reflecting as closely as possible the diversity in the community, giving them a short period of training, then fieldwork with and in the community. The methodology is geared to facilitating input from all, including those with low literacy levels. There have been some exploratory attempts to apply the methodology in regeneration projects in the North, and to build on it to take account of the higher base level of community capacity, for example, higher levels of education.

The 'how to' literature on PRA (eg, Theis and Grady, 1991) discusses various tools and

Hopscotch Asian Women's Centre

The Centre set up a course for young people to learn skills in community research and received Lottery Funding via the Save the Children Fund. Field research looked into problems of high unemployment and low achievement among local Bangladeshi young people. Trainees devised questionnaires, interviewed local Bangladeshi young people and training providers and employers. A report was produced. All trainees received payment for the course and were presented with certificates in recognition of the skills they had learnt.

The local authority, recognising that it was not reaching all sections of the community through its own methods, has increasingly used the Centre for consultation of other issues, for example, environmental policy, and for building up a picture of the area. The women are not just used as translators – they have found that they cannot just translate a document but have to put it in a language that people can understand and pull out the impact of the strategies on their day-to-day lives.

techniques, such as use of diagrams, annotated schematic maps or transects, ranking exercises, discussion of daily or annual cycle of tasks, group discussions, semi-structured interviews, use of reports, secondary sources and photos, and direct observation. The local fieldworkers themselves in the few days' initial training will be able to judge better than the outside 'experts' which techniques will work in their community, or to suggest new tools. Simple ideas are suggested, such as using different colours for noting data collection and analysis. Theis and Grady give many useful examples of successful projects and show examples of the data collected, along with brief guidelines for semi-structured interview techniques and other useful guidance.

- 'Planning for real' is another technique where participants focus on a model of the area and concentrate on the vision for the future. This has been used successfully in areas with large minority ethnic populations, such as in drawing up the Spitalfields People's Plan in East London.

- Focus groups are being increasingly used within regeneration. Birmingham City Council, for example, in its work on exclusion, is organising focus groups with specific sections of the population, for example, young Asian men, in order to gain more information on their particular experiences and needs.

- The establishment of sub- or theme-groups within the structures of participation, either at board level or as part of the consultative arrangements, is a further way of promoting good consultation and accessing a range of views. A number of partnerships have established women's and minority ethnic forums.

Issues in consultation

Studies have shown that there are various issues in consultation that need to be addressed in relation to working with diverse populations.

- Consensus is unlikely to emerge. Gregory (1998) found that in areas with minority groups, each group may see the behaviour of the others as threatening. Harrison et al (1995) found that greater attention should be given to the skills of conflict resolution for community development work in multiracial areas. They also recognised that while in some areas multi-ethnic organisations and consultation exercises might emerge, in others this was not possible. Consultation is a vital part of the process of community development and should not ignore conflict.

- It can raise false expectations in a community that needs are going to be met before funding has been secured to meet them. Care will need to be taken in how such exercises are presented to local people.

- Good practice guides exist. Zahno (1997), for example, provides a useful guide to working with the black voluntary sector and the DETR's *Involving the community in urban and rural regeneration* (DETR, 1997c) was updated in 1997 to cover ethnic minorities and faith communities. However, as May notes (1997), some of these guides are silent on gender issues such as those given below.

- Riseborough (1997) and May (1997) point out that women's time is not infinitely elastic and that the 'triple burden' of home, work and activism can restrict their capacity to become involved.

- Riseborough (1997) stresses the need for publicity and information on regeneration which actively refers to women's needs and concerns. As we have already seen for women and minority ethnic organisations, regeneration is often seen as not relevant or distant from the concerns of everyday life, especially where there is a heavy emphasis on physical regeneration and economic activity.

- Publicity should reflect the different routes to regeneration we have already mentioned. This can also assist in the process of moving groups to a more strategic view of regeneration. At a basic level photographs and publications should reflect the totality of the area's population. In relation to minority ethnic groups, providing information in appropriate languages is also important.

- Different mechanisms and strategies need to be used to ensure involvement of all. For example, the Women's Design Service has been working in SRBs in London on community health and safety audits. Despite a 'planning for real' exercise, in one borough there was little involvement of women with meetings mainly attracting Bangladeshi men. The Women's Design Service noted that meetings were held at five in the evening and there was no creche provided. They were organised by white men. Using different methods the Women's Design Service got 50 women to a tenants' hall in the daytime with a creche and other activities to attract women. As Riseborough (1997) states, "a paid women worker and a local place to meet make a difference to women's involvement".

Targets and outputs

If profiling and consultation are the first steps in implementing inclusive regeneration, the setting of targets for regeneration strategies and their monitoring is the next. In the present output-driven world of regeneration this is an essential issue and an important way in which present systems can be used to promote more inclusive regeneration. However, a number of factors need to be taken into consideration.

Targets: universal, specific or twin-tracking?

The issue of universal versus specific targets was raised in the opening chapter. The experience of regeneration has shown that some element of targeting is essential for issues of race to remain on the agenda and for gender to get there. However, twin-tracking can be useful to ensure acceptance of the strategy.

For example, a project may wish to address poverty and exclusion in its area. A simple target of increasing the income of the poorest 20% of the population by 10% over the lifetime of the project may appeal as a universal aim. Yet this could mean that the specific experience of men, women and ethnic minorities is ignored.

In profiling the area and establishing who the 20% are, it may well be found that women and ethnic minorities are over-represented and that many men have been excluded from the labour market long-term. As a result, targets could be set which could include training schemes, childcare places, and setting up a credit union to ensure that the overall objective is reached.

Methods of implementation

Delivering targets: implementation is also about delivering targets and managing projects. Examples, such as the work of the Women's Design Service and Hopscotch Women's Group show that involving a range of organisations in implementation is successful in promoting more gender and race aware regeneration. This should not be seen as confined to consultation and community development. For example, Oc et al (1997) revealed that there are many ethnic minority organisations skilled in providing training and business advice.

The dangers are that ethnic minority organisations or women's organisations can be restricted to delivering to their own communities instead of being seen as having universal skills, and efforts should be made to avoid this. Groups could also become diverted into meeting the regeneration agenda rather than the needs of their own members. Zahno (1997) also notes that organisations may need capacity building to take on contractual responsibilities.

Community development: community development has been identified in many studies as an important method of implementation in regeneration. There are, however, some dangers associated with a focus on community development. As Brownill et al (1996) showed in relation to Urban Development Corporations, it is easy for issues to do with race and gender to become marginalised within the community development section and not enter the mainstream of strategy. In this respect multiproject teams where, for example, those in a partnership working on employment promotion would have officers in those teams with responsibility for community development, race and gender, are maybe more appropriate.

For some areas, particularly with high numbers of Asian women, the employment of a woman from the same ethnic group may well be vital for ensuring any success in reaching women, as the Hopscotch case study has shown. Work with young men may similarly require 'gender-bonding'.

Resources: it goes without saying that all these activities mean resources need to be allocated to support them. Even small amounts can make an impact. Programmes which have had 'community chests' to provide small grants for one-off activities have been shown to be useful in building involvement. Funds for development work were vital in the success of the West Midlands capacity building bid outlined in the previous chapter.

Part of a process, not an end in itself: outcomes not outputs

The setting of targets can promote a mechanistic way of thinking, equating regeneration with the delivery of outputs. Studies have shown that targets need to be viewed as a means to an end and not just as a product in themselves. They are "the outward evidence of a process which has to go deeper" (CDF, 1997).

As this report has shown, inclusive regeneration is a process that runs through all stages of regeneration. Seeing outputs as part of such a process can lead to creativity in setting targets which will move this process forward. For example, taking the issue of consultation through the stages of such a process reveals the following:

Baseline survey: 60% of members of community organisations are women; 4% of responses to consultation exercises are from ethnic minority groups.

Targets set: responses to consultation from minority ethnic groups to reach 20% by year 1; community organisations to increase involvement of men in the area; ethnic minority forum to be set up.

Implementation: community development work; resource allocation; making information more accessible to minority ethnic groups.

Such an exercise could be repeated for all aspects of a partnership's activities.

Another way of looking at this is that projects should concentrate on outcomes and impacts rather than outputs. An output may be the delivery of training but the outcome may or may not be that the trainee gets a job. If she does, is this a low paid, temporary job or is it the first step to a rewarding career? The experience of negative impacts on intergroup relations arising

from the competitive bidding process has already been noted.

Many projects have long-term beneficial impacts that are difficult to set targets for (improved communication, cross-cultural understanding, better ability to work together, stronger pride in the area), a series of gains that could be summed up as capacities built. This difficulty means that attempts to find quantitative targets can often produce disappointing yields. As a result, various projects have called for qualitative outputs. For example, the Sandwell Capacity Building Programme mentioned in the previous chapter includes quantitative measures such as a 15% increase in the number of groups in the area and the establishment of a women's and an ethnic minority forum, but it also includes targets such as the input into decision making, the extent to which these forums are linked into other networks and cooperative action (LGIU, 1997).

Monitoring and impact analysis

The issue of outcomes as opposed to outputs has a bearing on the monitoring and evaluation of projects. According to the SRB bidding guidance:

> Ethnic monitoring must be undertaken to look at the extent to which members of ethnic minority groups are receiving benefits from the challenge fund assisted activities. (SRB Guidance Note No 2)

These requirements for ethnic monitoring represent an important advance over previous phases of urban policy. Yet, as the NCVO (1997) point out, outputs should reflect the profile/needs of different minority ethnic communities and women and other groups such as disabled people. Also, as Oc et al (1997) indicate, the experience of ethnic minority women in regeneration is very different from ethnic minority men. The Commission for Racial Equality (1997) provides a recommended classification based on the 1991 Census but also states that classifications should be appropriate to the local population; for example, it may be appropriate to break down the Black-African category in areas with Somali or francophone African residents. An example of one such locally specific classification drawn up by the

London Borough of Haringey is provided in Appendix A.

But as indicated above, quantitative data alone may not be adequate. Assessing the value of a community centre to a minority ethnic group, for example, may involve more than merely a head-count. Snap-shot surveys, interviews with users, participant observation could all provide a more accurate picture. The setting of qualitative targets such as those concerned with power and networking will also demand qualitative monitoring. This may mean asking every interested party to offer a view, participant observation of a range of key meetings and tracing case studies of key projects and decisions to assess who had greatest influence.

Widening involvement in these exercises can be another important method. As the Asian Women's Hopscotch Group has already shown there is scope for including community organisations in monitoring and evaluation. Research then itself becomes part of the process of regeneration and not a passive tool for observation.

Evaluation and regeneration research

The practice of evaluation and research is a final area where intervention to promote greater inclusivity has been proved to be effective. Information is vital for answering questions such as who is benefiting from regeneration policies, for spreading good practice on what works and what does not, and for establishing the challenges and benefits of various approaches.

It has been a constant theme of this report that many existing evaluations of urban regeneration, particularly those sponsored by government or major research institutions, have failed to adequately address such questions and so to move policy and practice forward. The benefits from the work that has been identified in this review need to be built on through a multilevel programme of research and evaluation, taking in the following.

Project evaluation.
Evaluation also looks at outcomes as well as outputs, and should be concerned with the effectiveness of regeneration and with issues of equity. Evaluation of projects is therefore needed alongside the official monitoring required for grant and other purposes. Evaluation can be effective in promoting inclusivity where:

- briefs to evaluators specify race and gender as areas of inquiry;

- the (usually) outside agency which undertakes evaluation has a track record in researching race and gender;

- attention is paid to involving all sections of the community in the evaluation through the techniques already outlined;

- measures are used not just to show what has happened, but to help understand how and why it happened.

A checklist for including a gender dimension to evaluation is included in Appendix B.

Identifying good practice.
The need for further identification and spreading of good practice in relation to implementing inclusive regeneration is vital. Many examples exist which are not finding their way through to the literature. Important areas where further research is needed include:

- the challenges and benefits of different approaches to inclusivity;

- detailed case study analysis of projects that made race and gender priority issues;

- the effectiveness of particular techniques such as PRA and the use of qualitative indicators and outputs;

- honest accounts of the conflicts and tensions of working in multi-ethnic areas.

National policy review and monitoring

Evaluations of the effectiveness of policy in tackling gender and race discrimination in regeneration are needed. The work of Loftman and Beazley (1998) in evaluating the operation of the SRB in relation to race is an important example of how such work can point to the marginalisation and exclusion that results from existing policies and practices. May (1997) calls for a gender audit of present and recent regeneration initiatives.

The Commission for Racial Equality (1997) provides a useful blueprint for national monitoring of the SRB to be undertaken by regional offices and national government. It includes the following:

- the proportion of outputs going to ethnic minorities in relation to all projected outputs;

- the proportion of outputs going to ethnic minorities under the main SRB objectives;

- the number and proportion of successful bids which specify

  - that they aim to benefit ethnic minorities;

  - that they have consulted ethnic minority organisations;

  - that key partners include ethnic minority organisations;

  - an ethnic minority organisation as a lead partner; and

  - that certain projects are specifically relevant to ethnic minorities.

Obviously such information would need disaggregating by specific ethnic groups and by gender. As the stress is on monitoring quantitative outputs, further research would be necessary to establish the outcomes of policy.

More research and evaluation is necessary along these lines. Only then can policy and practice develop a full repertoire of responses to the diversity in areas of regeneration.

5

Conclusions, summary and recommendations

This report has shown that issues of gender, race and diversity are at the core of regeneration practice and policy. It is impossible to understand the issues which regeneration is seeking to redress without an awareness of the relations of race and gender. Such a recognition needs to inform all levels of regeneration policy and practice as without it the aims of holistic, sustainable regeneration are impossible.

The report has also shown that there are many examples of inclusive regeneration being put into practice. This final chapter draws together the lessons from such initiatives in ways which can continue the present momentum. Firstly, different aspects of the regeneration process will be looked at. Secondly, specific recommendations will be made for the variety of actors in the regeneration game.

Building a new approach

This report has argued that bringing issues of race and gender from the margins to the mainstream is not about adding on to or making minor adjustments to existing agendas. It is about rethinking what regeneration means and how it is carried out. In particular, it means recognising that regeneration can mean different things to different people and therefore there are a diversity of routes to regeneration both for particular areas and for the diversity of people who live within them.

Overcoming marginality means recognising that inclusive regeneration must run throughout the whole regeneration process, as Table 8 shows. Inclusive strategies can start from a number of places: from bottom-up consultation with and

mapping of local areas; from pressure from local networks; and from committed policy makers.

By addressing inclusivity these recommendations are not suggesting that the implications for policy and practice of the different experiences of white and minority ethnic women and men are the same in every case. Rather, they are suggesting that there are ways of approaching policy which can open up possibilities but that more detailed analysis and thinking through of the details of policies and programmes is then necessary.

Finally, one of the findings of this report has been the *diversity between areas* in terms of factors for success, the dimensions of diversity and the strength of local organisation and commitment to tackling issues of race and gender. These recommendations therefore need to be adapted to the specific circumstances of particular areas.

Strategy and vision

There is a long history of blindness and marginalisation in policy in respect of race and particularly gender. However, the evidence in this report shows that diversity is a strategic regeneration issue in itself and in turn informs all other areas of regeneration policy.

- There is a need for an overall policy framework at the local, regional and national level which requires diversity to be addressed strategically.

- A mix of universal and specific strategies and targets should be used to translate such objectives into individual programmes (Coventry, p 20).

- 'Flagship' projects which address and celebrate diversity in areas should be considered in all regeneration programmes (Rich Mix, p 20).

- Mission statements and vision should place inclusivity at their core.

Locality profiling

Regeneration projects often ignore the diversity within their areas due to the inadequacy of information collected and available. This means that they cannot adequately assess needs and potential or devise and set appropriate strategies and targets. Each locality is different and to fully devise strategies and to assess the transferability or not of practice from other areas a diversity aware map of the local area is required. Therefore:

- a profile of the regeneration area should be drawn up using data disaggregated by gender, race and other aspects of diversity;

Table 8: Doing inclusive regeneration

Theme	Issues	Strategy
Baseline information	Ensuring full range of information is available	• Disaggregate information by race and gender • Ensure full range of community organisations covered • Consult with all sections of community • Use innovatory techniques involving diversity of organisations and residents
Vision and strategy	From the margins to the mainstream?	• National policy to make race and gender mandatory strategic objectives • Accept diversity of routes to regeneration • Diversity as an opportunity not a problem • Build on positive examples in current strategies
Partnerships	Silent partners Barriers to inclusion Hurdles of resource bidding process	• Equal opportunities 'badging' for partnerships • DETR/GORs to query bids lacking 'balance' • Support resources and mentoring for voluntary organisations to put in bids
Implementation	Inclusivity as process not just concept – implementation key targeting – universal or specific? Consultation and involvement	• Inclusive consultation more time for preparing bids • Community development • Race and gender 'experts' • Determine best mix of universal and specific targets • Share good practice
Regional and local infrastructure	Spatial variation in addressing issues of diversity Role of GORs Building strategic alliances and networks	• Capacity building for partnerships, GORs and voluntary organisations • Local networking at many levels to share experience • Accept universal aims appropriate in some areas, specific ones elsewhere
Monitoring, evaluation and research	Reviewing a silence Not mechanical exercise – part of inclusive process Appropriateness of indicators	• Government and research institute funding to ensure framework for evaluation includes race and gender • Case studies of good practice written up • Monitoring to include gender and recognise diversity in ethnic groups • Processes and outcomes not outputs • Use range of techniques: participatory, qualitative

- innovatory methods such as PRA and using local organisations and people to gather such information should be tried (Hopscotch, p 29);

- centralised collection and disaggregation of already available information, such as NOMIS, is a service which should be made available to individual partnerships and projects by organisations with the relevant resources.

Governance, partnerships and power

The literature on governance and regeneration reveals a contradictory potential for inclusivity:

- barriers to inclusion in networks and partnerships exist along lines of race and gender and are not countered by equal opportunities requirements;

- good practice guidelines on partnerships do not specify race and gender;

- there are insufficient lead partners which work exclusively around diversity;

- a seat at the table does not necessarily translate into power and influence as some voices are more powerful than others and styles of power within partnerships can exclude full participation;

- processes of governance such as speed and the emphasis on outputs can have a negative impact on inclusivity;

- yet where lead partners are proactive, local organisations are well organised and there are committed officers, partnerships can open up routes to influence.

Therefore:

- partnerships should be required to comply with 'equal opportunities badging' (Greenwich, p 24);

- partnership membership should be monitored and places reserved for organisations representing diverse voices (Greenwich, p 24);

- members should be chosen for their skills, not just because of their race or gender;

- training and capacity building for all partners should include exercises relating to race and gender awareness as a way of building trust and understanding between partners and recognising where styles of operating can be exclusionary (Appendix C);

- capacity building for less powerful partners should be undertaken (Sandwell, p 26);

- regional and local infrastructure and networks should be created (West Midlands, p 25)

Implementation

All aspects of the implementation of regeneration need to be looked at through the prism of inclusivity. In particular, several studies have highlighted issues of community development and capacity building as important for securing race and gender awareness in practice. The focus on outputs as opposed to outcomes must be reconsidered; however, there are few examples as yet of the outcomes and impacts of inclusive regeneration. Imaginative methods for setting targets and monitoring these can be a useful part of an inclusive process. Recommendations include:

- consultation practices should ensure widespread involvement;

- information should be made relevant to and understandable by all within the locality;

- a mix of universal and specific targets should be set which address diversity;

- where universal targets are set their race and gender implications and impacts must be analysed, sub-targets set where appropriate and implementation strategies specified;

- monitoring should be by gender and race;

- good practice guidelines need to include race and gender;

- greater focus on outcomes not outputs;

- innovative methods for monitoring outcomes including qualitative measures and the involvement of residents;

- greater involvement of ethnic minority and women's organisations in delivering regeneration outcomes.

Evaluation and research

Throughout this particular research the lack of research and evaluation has been identified as a major barrier to promoting inclusive regeneration. Without a full assessment of the differential impact of regeneration policy, who benefits and the thorough identification and dissemination of good practice, marginalisation will remain. Research must be gender and race aware to encompass the complexity of regeneration. Therefore:

- government and or major research funders should commission a gender and race audit of current policy and practice;

- once major programmes are complete, such as the Joseph Rowntree Area Regeneration Programme (of which this report is part), there should be a critical overview of all research undertaken to bring together findings on and implications for greater inclusivity;

- more funding is needed for research which evaluates good practice in race, gender and regeneration and its dissemination;

- there should be wider dissemination of the valuable work (largely from the voluntary sector) already carried out on good practice.

Recommendations for regeneration actors

To community and voluntary organisations

- Form and build networks at the local and regional level to ensure participation and to increase their influence over policy.

- Form strategic alliances with other agencies as, for example, mentors to increase their opportunities for involvement in regeneration and for success in bidding.

GORs/Regional Development Agencies

- Develop a regional regeneration strategy which addresses and prioritises issues of diversity.

- Require all successful bids to show evidence of implementing this strategy.

- Carry out outreach work and seminars to publicise regeneration initiatives.

- Give support to bids which prioritise race and gender.

- Give support to women only or black-led bidders.

- Encourage partnerships with potential between different rounds.

- Monitor membership of partnerships and use delivery plans to set inclusive targets.

- Encourage inter-GOR sharing of good practice.

- Widen present monitoring requirements to include outcomes and impacts.

- Research and disseminate good practice.

Partnerships

As agencies of governance

- All partnerships to adopt equal opportunities policies.

- 'Badging' in partnerships to include equal opportunities.

- Membership to be monitored and targets set for increased representativeness.

- All partners to undergo training and capacity building to recognise each other's strengths and to maximise participation.

As bidders and delivery mechanisms

- Encourage a diversity of partners.

- Provide the necessary support to organisations who want to become partners.

- Involve women's and ethnic minority organisations in delivering outputs.

- Use the setting of output targets to promote inclusive regeneration.

- Incorporate community development as a key part of regeneration and use imaginative methods in consultation, research and evaluation.

- Evaluation and monitoring to address outcomes and impacts.

Government

- Take a lead to ensure that regeneration is inclusive.

- Make the strategic objective on benefiting ethnic minorities compulsory in current or future policy.

- Introduce a similar strategic objective for gender.

- Make inclusivity a theme for priority in future bidding rounds and ensure adequate resources.

- Continue the shift in emphasis from competition to need.

- Set up a group in the DETR to progress these issues and commission a race and gender audit of regeneration policy.

- Ringfence resources for specific groups.

Finally...

The limitations of spatial policy should be recognised. It is impossible for local policies alone to reverse disadvantage and discrimination. This is especially true in relation to race and gender where attitudes and prejudices spring from wider society. It is equally true of local economies in a global era. Nevertheless, by looking at regeneration through the perspective of diversity not only will the life-chances of many in those areas be improved but the goal of sustainable regeneration is likely to become closer.

Central to this is the acceptance that there are diverse routes to regeneration. The 'rich mix' that results builds on the full range of resources and potential in regeneration areas by, in the words of the Rich Mix Centre itself, "unleashing energy". Diversity is an opportunity not a threat and a strength not a weakness. Regeneration therefore becomes as much an issue of "nurturing different capabilities and forms of governance" (Gilroy, 1996) as about delivering outputs.

References and further reading

[Those references marked * and briefly annotated are key texts.]

Atkinson, R. and Moon, G. (1994) *Urban policy in the UK*, London: Macmillan.

Brownill, S. (1993) *Developing London's Docklands*, 2nd edn, London: Paul Chapman.

Brownill, S. (1997) 'Regen(d)eration: women and urban policy in the UK', Paper given at 'Women and the City Conference', Oxford Brookes University, September.

Brownill, S., Razzaque, K., Stirling, T. and Thomas, H. (1996) 'Local government and the racialisation of urban policy in the UK: the case of Urban Development Corporations', *Urban Studies*, vol 33, no 8, pp 1337-55.

BTEG (1996) *The West Midlands black voluntary sector regional regeneration network: Single Regeneration Budget Challenge Fund bid*, London: BTEG.

BTEG (1997) *A strategy for ensuring black communities are involved in regeneration*, London: BTEG.

Campbell, B. (1993) *Goliath*, London: Methuen.

CDF (Community Development Foundation) (1997) *Guidelines to the community involvement aspects of the SRB Challenge Fund*, London: CDF.

Coventry City Council (1998) *Coventry Community Plan*, Coventry: Coventry City Council.

CRE (Commission for Racial Equality) (1997) *SRB Challenge Fund: Action for racial equality*, London: CRE.

*Crook, J. (1995) *Silent partners: The impact of the SRB on black communities*, London: BTEG. [Critical analysis of the first round of the SRB concentrating on the way the operation of the Challenge Fund excluded minority groups.]

CURS (Centre For Urban and Regional Studies) (1998: forthcoming) *The SRB: A review of Challenge Fund Round III*, Birmingham: CURS.

Darke, J. and Rowland, V. (1997) 'The role of women in tenant management: the case of Kensington and Chelsea', Paper given at 'Women and the City Conference', Oxford, September.

DETR (Department of the Environment, Transport and the Regions) (1997a) *Bidding guidance for Round 4 of the SRB Challenge Fund*, London: DoE.

DETR (1997b) *Effective partnerships. A handbook for members of SRB Challenge Fund Partnerships*, London: DoE.

DETR (1997c) *Involving the community in urban and rural regeneration: A guide for practitioners*, London: DETR.

DETR (1997d) *Regeneration programmes: The way forward*, London: DETR.

DETR (1997e) *SRB Challenge Fund Round 4: Supplementary Guidance*, London: DoE.

DoE (Department of the Environment) (1994) *Assessing the impact of urban policy*, London: HMSO.

DoE (1996) *Interim evaluation of City Challenge*, London: HMSO.

Eade, J. (1998) 'Global processes and customised landscapes', *Rising East*, vol 1, no 31, pp 52-73.

Geddes, M. (1997) *Partnership against poverty and exclusion? Local regeneration strategies and excluded communities in the UK*, Bristol: The Policy Press.

Gilroy, R. (1996) 'Building routes to power', *Local Economy*, vol 11, no 3, pp 248-58.

Goode, J., Callender, C. and Lister, R. (1998) *Purse or wallet? Gender inequalities and income distribution within familes on benefits*, London: Policy Studies Institute.

Gregory, S. (1998) *Transforming local services*, York: York Publishing Services.

Hall, S., Beazley, M., Bentley, G., Burfitt, A., Collinge, C., Lee, P., Loftman, P., Nevin, B. and Srbljania, A. (1996) *The SRB: A review of Challenge Fund Round II*, Birmingham: CURS.

Harrison, L., Hoggett, P. and Jeffers, S. (1995) 'Race, ethnicity and community development', *Community Development Journal*, vol 30, no 2, April, pp 144-57.

Hastings, A., McArthur, A. and McGregor, A. (1996) *Less than equal? Community organisations and estate regeneration partnerships*, Bristol: The Policy Press.

Hoggett, P., Jeffers, S. and Harrison, L. (1994) 'Reflexivity and uncertainty in the research process', *Policy and Politics*, vol 22, no 1, pp 59-70.

LBGU (London Boroughs Grants Unit) (1997) *Vision and visibility: Regeneration and ethnic minority communities in London*, London: LBGU.

LGIU (Local Government Information Unit) (1994) *Women and urban regeneration*, London: LGIU.

LGIU (1995) *Race and regeneration: A consultation document*, London: LGIU.

LGIU (1997) *Capacity building programme for urban regeneration: Sandwell Case Study*, London: LGIU.

*Loftman, P. and Beazley, M. (1998) *Race and regeneration: A review of the SRB Challenge Fund*, London: LGIU. [Critically analyses the operation of the SRB in relation to race and strategic priorities, resources and involvement in partnerships. Useful case studies of bids in which ethnic minority organisations have been in the lead or key partners. Identifies barriers to inclusion and makes recommendations to government and GORs to overcome them.]

London Borough of Greenwich (1994) *Survey of ethnic minority employment needs in the Greenwich Waterfront area*, London: LBG.

London Borough of Haringey (1996) *Assuring racial equality in SRB Bids*, London: LBH.

London Borough of Tower Hamlets (nd) *The Rich Mix Centre for London*, London: LBTH.

LRN (London Regeneration Network) (1997) *Report of survey into SRB board composition*, London: LRN.

McCabe, A., Lowndes, V. and Skelcher, C. (1997) *Partnerships and networks: An evaluation and development manual*, York: York Publishing Services.

McCulloch, A. (1997) 'You've fucked up the estate and now you're carrying a briefcase', in P. Hoggett (ed) *Contested communities: Experiences, struggles, policies*, Bristol: The Policy Press.

MacFarlane, R. (1993) *Community involvement in City Challenge. A good practice guide*, London: NCVO.

Mawson, J., Beazley, M., Burfitt, A., Collinge, C., Hall, S., Loftman, P., Nevin, B. and Srbljania, A. (1995) *The SRB: The stocktake*, Birmingham: CURS.

*May, N. (1997) *Challenging assumptions: Gender assumptions in urban regeneration*, York: York Publishing Services. [Clear and well-argued case for a gender aware approach to urban regeneration. Concentrates on gender and poverty and on drawing on examples from Oxfam's work in the South. Emphasises strategic approaches and tools for capacity building.]

Modood, T., Berthoud, R., Lakey, J., Nazroo, J., Smith, P., Virdee, S. and Beishon, S. (1997) *Ethnic minorities in Britain*, London: Policy Studies Institute.

Munt, I. (1994) 'Race, urban policy and urban problems', in H. Thomas and V. Krishnarayan (eds) *Race equality and planning: Policies and procedures*, Aldershot: Avebury.

NCVO (National Council For Voluntary Organisations) (1997) *Further to go: An assessment of the 1996/97 SRB Challenge Fund approvals and their impact on voluntary and community organisations*, London: NCVO.

*Oc, T., Tiesdell, S. and Moynihan, D. (1997) *Urban regeneration and ethnic minority groups: Training and business support in City Challenge areas*, Bristol, The Policy Press. [Analyses skills training and business support needs of ethnic minorities, with an awareness of the differences between the various minority groups and the specific needs of women.]

ONS (Office for National Statistics) (1997) *Living in Britain*, London: The Stationery Office.

Power, A. and Tunstall, R. (1997) *Dangerous disorder: Riots and violent disturbances in thirteen areas of Britain, 1991-92,* York: York Publishing Services.

*Riseborough, M. (1997) *The gender report: Women and regional regeneration in the Midlands. A research report of SRB Round III Bids in the region*, Birmingham: CURS. [Reports on surveys carried out in the West Midlands on gender and the SRB. Includes a preliminary analysis of national data on the SRB. Shows the low priority given to gender with the SRB and raises issues about women's involvement in SRB partnerships.]

SIA (1994) *From City Challenge to the SRB: A black perspective*, London: SIA.

Skelcher, C., McCabe, A., Lowndes, V. with Nanton, P. (1996) *Community networks in urban regeneration: "it all depends who you know"*, Bristol: The Policy Press.

Stewart, M. and Taylor, M. (1995) *Empowerment and estate regeneration: A critical review*, Bristol: The Policy Press.

Taylor, M. (1995) *Unleashing the potential: Bringing residents to the centre of regeneration*, York: Joseph Rowntree Foundation.

Thake, S. (1995) *Staying the course: The role and structures of community regeneration organisations*, York: York Publishing Services.

Theis, J. and Grady, H.M. (1991) *Participatory rapid appraisal for community development: A training manual based on experiences in the Middle East and North Africa*, London: International Institute for Environment and Development and Save the Children Fund.

Thomas, H., Brownill, S., Stirling, T. and Razzaque, K. (1995) 'Theory, race equality and urban policy evaluation', *Race Equality and Local Governance Paper No 1*, Department of City and Regional Planning, University College Cardiff and School of Planning, Oxford Brookes University.

Tilson, B., Mawson, J., Beazley, M., Burfitt, A., Collinge, C., Hall, S., Loftman, P., Nevin, B. and Srbljania, A. (1997) 'Partnerships for regeneration: The Single Regeneration Budget Challenge Fund Round One', *Local Government Studies*, vol 23, no 1, pp 1-15.

Valentine, G. (1990) 'Women's fear and the design of public space', *Built Environment*, vol 16, no 4, pp 288-303.

Williams, S. with Seed, J. and Mwau, A. (1994) *The Oxfam gender training manual*, Oxford: Oxfam.

Wilson, A. and Charlton, K. (1997) *Making partnerships work*, York: York Publishing Services.

Women's Design Service (1997) *The good practice manual on tenant participation*, London: WDS.

*Zahno, K. (1997) *Working with the black voluntary sector: A good practice guide*, London: Pan London Regeneration Consortium. [Discusses the potential roles of the black voluntary sector within regeneration partnerships. Sets out the diversity within the black voluntary sector and provides useful case studies of actual involvement in regeneration.]

Glossary

Asian, black

When anti-racist strategies in local authorities were being adopted in the mid-1980s, it became common practice to use the word 'black' to refer to all ethnic groups that were not white, as a political strategy that emphasised their common experience of living in a white-dominated racist society. Such usage is no longer generally acceptable as it masks the specific experiences of Asians. The politics of identity as well as recent research emphasises the different trajectories of groups with different origins. Many people of South Asian descent prefer to use phrases such as 'black and Asian' or 'black and minority ethnic' (BME). However, the earlier usage of the word 'black' is retained in organisational titles such as Black Training and Enterprise Group and in references to the black voluntary sector. It must be remembered that these include diverse minority groups.

Capacity building

This can apply both to communities and to individuals. It refers to a range of capacities: an understanding of the structures of governance and how to get access to them, effectiveness in committee roles, skills for setting up and sustaining grassroots organisations, motivating others, getting and keeping a job, bringing in resources, challenging harmful stereotypes, working with diversity. Men and women and different ethnic groups may have different priorities in capacity building.

Citizenship see Social exclusion

Community

This word refers to something shared which may be a territory and/or a common ethnicity, common interest etc. It is often used ideologically to imply that fellow residents in a locality should have common interests and friendly interactions. This *may* be the case or there may be several communities occupying the same territory. Creating positive relationships within an area may be a meaningful goal but aiming to create 'community spirit' is too vague to be useful.

Diversity

The word diversity is being increasingly used in regeneration circles and in the wider policy area. It has become popular as a 'catch-all' concept to sum up the fact that populations and cultures are made up of a wide range of communities of interest as opposed to a geographical population having common interests. These interest groups can include: black and ethnic minorities, women and men, younger people and/or students and many more. As with other 'universal' terms such as exclusion there are advantages to the term as a way to get issues on to the policy agenda and to begin to break through the tendency to single issue thinking: a box on gender, a box on race. But it can diminish the importance of specific aspects of institutional discrimination and unequal power within a society.

Empowerment

This is similar to capacity building but carries greater connotations of an individual's or community's sense of their own growing power. This can produce excitement and energy which can then be used to move further, and is particularly strong if those concerned have previously been labelled as lacking particular qualities due to their gender or ethnicity.

However, it has been argued (Harrison et al, 1995) that empowerment is a culturally relative value, and that some groups may choose to allow others to take decisions on their behalf.

Ethnicity, ethnic groups

In order to avoid the use of the term 'race' which lacks a scientific referent we use the term ethnicity although this too is controversial. Everyone has some sort of ethnic identity, based on being raised within and identifying with a group that has specific norms, customs and beliefs. These cultural practices are themselves changing as individuals and families make choices about how to run their lives. Like gender roles, ethnicities are structures that are open to negotiation.

There are many ethnic groups in Britain and any ethnic classification is to an extent an arbitrary compromise; however, the differences referred to have a more substantiated reality than those supposedly denoted by 'race'. The classification used in the 1991 Census is open to criticism on various counts, not least the absence of any 'mixed' categories and the treatment of 'white' as undifferentiated. In a specific regeneration area a project would need to understand what ethnic differences are accorded social significance within that area, while keeping another eye on the desirability of having information which is comparable to that from other projects.

The choices made about how to be a member of a particular group that is living in Britain will be patterned in systematic ways: research has examined how lifestyles vary with length of time in Britain, being born in Britain or overseas, educational level, gender and so on.

There may be distinctive values and patterns of social solidarity, for example, based on religious observance or extended family networks, that serve as survival or coping strategies. It has sometimes been the case that differences within and between minority groups have been ignored by regeneration projects. As the tables in Chapter 1 show, levels of employment, earnings, family structures and the housing situation show great variation: for example, comparing those of Bangladeshi origin and African Asians.

An increasing number of British people have mixed ancestry: in most cases they are regarded as a member of an ethnic minority group rather than as white (if that is part of their ancestry) but the experience of multiple ethnic identity (and a degree of choice) is not confined to this group. Modood et al (1997) show that most members of minority groups regard themselves as British *and* Indian, Pakistani, Jamaican or whatever other affiliation they feel.

The significance of gender divisions varies between ethnic groups: see *Race and gender* below. In particular there is great variation in the extent to which women's behaviour is controlled by men. A recent report on urban regeneration and ethnic minority groups called for policies to "recognise and respond to the fact that ethnic minority women are often further disadvantaged because of cultural attitudes of many ethnic groups" (Oc et al, 1997, p viii).

Household structure

	White	Caribbean	Indian and African Asian	Pakistani/ Bangladeshi
1-2 adults	59	42	20	12
1 adult + child(ren)	5	17	3	3
2 adults, 1-2 child(ren)	15	19	26	14
2 adults, 3 or more children	4	5	9	21
3 + adults with/without children	17	18	42	49

Source: Modood et al (1997, Tables 2.16)

Although there are many different groups within the category 'white', including some which have faced severe discrimination, the experience of racism will inevitably be stronger for those who can be distinguished by their appearance. Racism may take the form of stereotyped assumptions as well as prejudice and hatred.

Ethnically blind, ethnically aware

As with gender blind/aware, but in relation to ethnicity.

Gender

Briefly, gender refers to the rules of appropriate behaviour for men and women that we learn from multiple influences throughout our lives. The starting point for a consideration of gender in regeneration is the fact that poverty and deprivation affect women and men differently (May, 1997). More women than men are in poverty; households headed by women are particularly likely to be poor; women's wages are lower than men's. This applies not only to lone mothers but to most elderly women.

In many disadvantaged areas we see men and women coping with poverty in different ways. For some men crime may be a means of acquiring goods they cannot afford to buy. Other men may choose merely to avoid any activities defined as the women's sphere. For women, coping may be more on the level of survival and solidarity (Campbell, 1993). Women have been described as the glue that holds urban areas together, through their greater involvement in active citizenship, their networks with other women, for example, to share childcare, and their efforts to keep families together and neighbourhoods tolerable to live in.

But because this is what women are supposed to do, this role goes unnoticed – unless it breaks down or is perceived to be problematic, as has happened in the case of single mothers. It is impossible to understand these different experiences without reference to the ideas of *gender*.

A working definition of gender: people are born female or male, but learn to be girls and boys who grow up into women and men. They are taught what the appropriate behaviour and attitudes, roles and activities are for them, and how they should relate to other people. This learned behaviour is what makes up gender identity, and determines gender roles. (Williams et al, 1994)

Gender is thus about social roles, behaviour and relationships. As with any social role, the 'rules' are synthesised from a multiplicity of sources, and the individual may feel comfortable with or resist these rules. The rules are not rigid: people have choices about how to be a man or a woman. They also change over time. These changes are not entirely voluntaristic: economic restructuring has removed the possibility of a secure job-for-life providing sufficient income to support a family, particularly for manual workers. Women know that they cannot expect lifelong economic support from a man.

Gender roles vary not only with time but also between cultures. Different societies will allow different degrees of choice for women in how they organise their lives, and this can be seen across different ethnicities in Britain. Gender roles are not symmetrical; there has always been unequal power, with men prescribing how women should behave. Women or men who 'break the rules' about gender behaviour face social disapproval, with ridicule, violence or ostracism among the methods used by others to try to restore their sense of the social world as it should be.

Because of the way roles are learnt and sanctioned, they are internalised. If women are oppressed it is not just by the behaviour of men they interact with now: it is from the cumulative effect of their own learning from women as well as from men. Thus women experience material and ideological disadvantage. The tables in Chapter 1 show that women are worse paid than men and less likely to be in full-time work; this means that they are more likely to live in rented accommodation and in poor areas.

Gender blind and gender aware

Gender blind describes an attitude where gender differences are not seen or are accorded no significance. For example, a youth worker may fail to notice that some activities are monopolised by boys or treat different gender preferences as natural. Gender aware practice involves constant mental checking of gender differentials in who participates, who benefits and who is excluded.

Networks

Networks can be defined as informal connections linking some or all of the variety of agencies and interests involved in regeneration (Skelcher et al 1996). While they do not have the same decision making and implementation role as partnerships, networks can become formalised into partnerships. Networks also have an important role in influencing local and regional policy and sharing information and good practice at a variety of levels.

Partnerships

The delivery and governance mechanism for regeneration projects, a typical partnership will include one or more local authorities, a training provider, agencies in the voluntary sector and representatives of local residents.

Race and racism

See the entry on *Ethnicity*. The concept of race has no scientific basis: the phenotypes (appearance) on which racial classifications are based are not distinctive and do not predict individual qualities. However, the widespread though mistaken belief that race *is* significant and the prejudices based on supposed racial differences gives rise to racism. Racism thus includes discrimination based on stereotyping as well as extreme manifestations such as violence.

Race and gender

The combination of gender and ethnicity is not simply additive: the meaning of being a man or a women is different in different cultures, and women's subordination takes a different typical form in each. Women in the Muslim communities tend to be constrained (or protected) by patriarchal family structures with a polarised set of gender role expectations.

Caribbean women are much less likely to be under the control of male partners or fathers although they are quite likely to have the double burden of employment combined with childrearing. White women and those of Indian, African Asian or Chinese descent are somewhere between these extremes, with the two latter groups particularly likely to be bearing a dual burden.

Regeneration and renewal

Regeneration is a word that is used frequently, but rarely defined. It is open to various interpretations by different actors and interests. Residents may have a different view of what constituents 'regeneration' than policy makers. Literally, regeneration means new growth or healing, in urban regeneration, to an area seen as damaged physically and socially. It implies active agency by residents in an area, helped by outside professionals. By contrast, renewal could be applied to an area without involving residents.

Social exclusion

This term as a near-synonym for poverty has been introduced by the European Community. It implies not only poverty but barriers to full participation in society due to lack of personal resources and skills, and/or the prejudices of others. Exclusion may be economic (poverty), social (avoidance or marginalisation) or political (disenfranchisement or apathy). It is the converse of citizenship. Groups that are subject to discrimination may thereby be socially excluded.

Voluntary sector

This refers to non-profit making bodies having an unpaid management committee, usually with each organisation having a focused and quasi-charitable objective: to provide affordable rented housing, to support community arts.

Appendix A: Checklist on equal opportunities in preparing SRB bids

(London Borough of Haringey, 1996)

Checklist of equal opportunities categories

[*Authors' note:* Haringey's checklist on preparing bids would be relevant in any locality, but their list of categories for ethnic monitoring was developed to reflect the particular groups living in that borough. Those in other areas should develop their own list in consultation with communities in their area.]

London Borough of Haringey, summary and checklist

A. About the bid

Projects developed and run by or for the Council should explicitly recognise the diverse nature of the community and the Council's commitment to serving all sections of Haringey's community.

1. Is the bid appropriate for equal opportunities issues?

2. Does the statement of objective embed the notion of inclusiveness?

B. Consultation and participation

Officers in preparing bids should consult and work closely with the local community in the areas of benefit of the bids, ensuring that programmes are put together, delivered and managed in a way that reflect and respond to local needs.

3. Did you consult with local people in the area of benefit of the bid about:

   i the content of the bid?

   ii the management of the project?

4. What input did local people have in preparing the bid?

5. Any arrangements for reporting back progress to local people in the area of benefit?

6. Did consultation include people from minority groups?

C. Partnerships

The concept of partnership with the community plays a crucial role in SRB. Where a partnership arrangement is required, officers should routinely explore ways of bringing in organisations representing minority community interests into full participation.

7. Is the bid in partnership with other agencies?

8. Are those agencies committed to equal opportunities?

   (There must be evidence such as written policy and structures to substantiate a 'yes' answer.)

9. Are you aware of the Council's guideline 'CCT and equalities'?

10. Were you influenced by that document in awarding the contracts relating to the bid?

11. Does the partnership include agencies of ethnic minority origin?

12. What efforts were made to secure ethnic minority participation in the bid?

D. Monitoring arrangements

SRB Guidance Notes place emphasis on ethnic monitoring and review. Monitoring arrangements must be in place to ensure that enough appropriate information is generated to measure the extent to which projects are benefiting all sections of the community, and where projects are specifically targeted, to measure the extent to which the target groups have benefited.

Haringey's own equalities classification should be used to reflect fully the borough ethnic composition.

13. Are there arrangements for monitoring the process and outcomes of the project, including the ethnicity of the actual beneficiaries?

14. Do the monitoring arrangements include the use of Haringey's own equal opportunities classifications?

E. Specific provision

One of the SRB objectives is 'to promote initiatives of benefit to ethnic minorities'. This suggests inclusion of specific provision within the SRB bid, aimed at addressing the specific needs of ethnic minorities.

15. Are there any specific provisions within the bid targeted at a minority ethnic community?

F. Equal opportunities health check of bids

Internal appraisal of bids prior to local approval should include an equal opportunities health check. The Council has an 'Equal Opportunities Checklist on Project Definition, Implementation and Evaluation' for guiding its mainstream projects.

16. Were you influenced by that document in developing the bid?

(DoE and Haringey classifications are given below)

DoE	Haringey
White	UK European
Black Caribbean	Greek Cypriot
Black African	Turkish Cypriot
Black Other	African
Indian Sub-Continent	Caribbean/West Indian
Chinese Vietnamese	Indian Asian
Other ethnic group	Pakistani Asian
Not specific	Bangladeshi Asian
	East African Asian
	Other Asian
	Irish
	Women
	People with disabilities
	Other

DoE classifications differ from Haringey's in that they do not view the Irish, and people of Mediterranean origin, that is, Turkish, Greek, Cypriot, as separate ethnic categories. Haringey's classifications do, and make further distinctions in regard to the 'Asian' category.

The two classifications are not incompatible although the exclusive use of the DoE's will fail to pick up a number of minority communities which nevertheless form a significant proportion of Haringey's population. We therefore recommend that for all SRB bids, Haringey's own classifications be used. The resulting information could then be aggregated to generate the information for the DoE classifications.

Appendix B: Checklist proposed by Oxfam (1995)

Key questions in consultation, planning and evaluation

1. Why are women disadvantaged in the programme or project area? Why are they unable to develop their potential effectively?

2. When is it best to consult women? At which time of the day/week/year do they have the most time? When will they be able to engage in project activities?

3. Where is it best to meet the women?

4. Who has been consulted? Whose views have been incorporated into decisions? Who has been left out?

5. What are the practical and strategic needs of the women in the project or programme area, identified by themselves? identified by the intermediary agency?

6. How can the different views on needs be incorporated into project plans? How are they going to be addressed? How can women's needs best be met? How can men's needs be met without harming women?

7. What do women themselves hope to achieve from a project? Have they been asked? How long do they expect it to take? Are their aspirations realistic? Are their aims the same as those of the donor agency?

8. Is there resistance to considering gender issues among the members of the implementing agency? How can this be dealt with?

9. Does the project proposal show evidence of an understanding of the different roles and activities of women and men? Is it clear who uses and who controls which resources, and who controls project benefits?

10. How will gender sensitivity be built into project or programme monitoring and evaluation? Have clear guidelines and criteria been drawn up from the start?

11. What is the situation of women nationally and regionally? Does the project address the situation of women in the project area within this context?

12. The following specific points should always be addressed:

    Time (women are rarely at rest): do they have more time or less time on their hands now than before? Is this because of or in spite of the project? Why?

    Money to spend (women often have problems of access to cash): do they have more or less money to spend on household and children than before?

    Money to spend on themselves (poor women rarely spend money on themselves).

    Physical health (poor women have heavy workloads).

    Stress levels.

    Confidence: Do they have more or less confidence in their abilities to cope than they did before?

    Changes: hoped for or unforeseen?

    Has anyone suffered from the project?

    Is the project sustainable? What are the constraints? What can be done about them? by whom?

Appendix C: Training session: barriers to partnership

(Source: McCabe et al, 1997)

Networks and partnerships: training exercises

Membership and barriers

Introduction

Networks may appear to be 'open' arrangements with few barriers to involvement. Yet, as with more formal partnerships, networks may have a restricted, if changing, membership. Blocks to participation can exist – although go unrecognised. In other words, one person's network is another person's clique.

Exercise

The following exercise uses quotations from network members and those involved in formal partnerships. These have been selected to stimulate thought and comment on both the nature of networks and partnerships and the barriers to participation.

The exercise may be used in two ways:

- on an individual basis to encourage those involved to reflect on the nature of their own networks and partnerships;

- as a training tool.

If used during a training session:

1. Provide all participants with the 'general comments' on networks and partnerships (all quotes can be used, or just selected comments).

2. Break into small groups. Ask participants to consider:

- whether the comments apply to their networks/partnerships

- if so, why? if not, why not?

- whether they agree/disagree with statements and why.

3. Gather general feedback.

4. Break into groups and provide each group with a set of statements on barriers to participation based on:

- resources

- class and community

- gender

- race.

5. Feedback: the final feedback/plenary should invite action plan proposals for overcoming barriers to participation.

Key learning issues/questions

- Differing attitudes/experiences of networks and partnerships.

- The variety of barriers to participation.

- The influence of resources, race, gender, class/community, on participation in networks and partnerships.

- Factors influencing inclusion in, and exclusion from networks and partnerships.

- Action points for overcoming barriers to participation.

- The extent to which membership of networks/partnerships may be based on personal values.

See also:

- Chapter 2, *Accountability and representation*
- Chapter 3, *Levels of involvement*
- Chapter 4, *Characteristics of networks and partnerships*

- Chapter 4, *Mapping networks*

[Time required: 1-1.5 hours]

Class and community

"In all the work I've been involved in, it's us who have had to put the effort into reaching the Council's level. We've always had to come up to their level. They never came down to ours, so you're disadvantaged two ways." "The parameters and nature of participation [in the partnership] is not always clear. Local authorities need to ask what they are expecting of people – are we inviting in people who have had no previous contact with bureaucratic structures and asking them to work at the same place as practitioners? If so, what are we offering by way of support?" "Community representatives in the partnerships have gained greater assertiveness and confidence through knowing the right people and processes." "You can easily get community representation [in partnership] wrong. You can get the wrong people – the people who shout loudest are not necessarily those with community support."

Race

"Black networks are very much there – but operate quite possibly on a different basis." "In the voluntary sector there is a clique of people who get access to funds. They are people who have been around for a long time.... Black organisations are on the outside because the networks say 'we are dubious about working with them'." "I'm sick of being asked to sit on partnership boards as 'the voice of the Black community'. Is just such a token gesture." "It's [the partnership's] responsibility is that the democratic process is gone through right down the line. It's not a matter of the Race Equality Council being asked to pick two tried and tested people to sit on the Partnership Board and represent people."

Gender

"Although things have changed ... [network] relationships are based on gender, not on other primary concerns." "Women's networks tend to be organic and often invisible in the workplace and, if recognised, they are seen as threatening or trivialised." "Men don't need reasons to get together. We fought for our slice of the employment cake, but at the same time did not pass on childcare to men." "[Black women] are not networked with other groups; there's a lack of social connections beyond our own culture."